Praise for *Be*

"***Beyond Common*** is exactly what this book will teach any person at any level of business. How to set yourself apart and be memorable. Personally, and professionally, success is about creating and building human connections and that is what this book helps you master."

John R. DiJulius III–*Author of The Relationship Economy -Building Stronger Customer Connections in the Digital Age*

"When I met Tracey, one of the first things she told me was that her goal in life was to support women and help them be the best versions of themselves. It doesn't surprise me that she took that enthusiasm and her knowledge from the beauty industry and turned it into such an engaging and thoughtful book. ***Beyond Common*** is a great read for anyone looking to grow personally and professionally."

Amy Wong–*President of Dot Org Solutions*

"Tracey is one of those people that you want to be around because she makes you want to be a better person. She is inspiring in her professionalism and in the way she is genuinely a kind and caring person. Tracey brings out the best in people by being an example of strength, confidence, as well as being just an all-around bad ass. Her vast experience as a business owner, motivational speaker, hairdresser, teacher, and coach make her the best person to teach what it is to be ***Beyond Common***."

Jennifer Panlilio–*Master Hairstylist & Financial Advisor*

"A true industry innovator, Tracey, is a natural born leader. Authentic & passionate are two words that resonate with me. Her continuous quest for knowledge is one of her biggest assets in helping those she leads to succeed!"

Jen LeBlanc–Director of Marketing and Operations
at Salon Rootz

"Tracey's no-nonsense approach to professionalism catches your attention and moves you to keep reading. Using her own mistakes as a vehicle for reflection, Tracey's candor enables the reader to do the same. After reading this book, you too will strive to become **Beyond Common**."

Patrice Blakemore–Business Service Advisor
Goldman Sachs 10,000 Small Businesses

"Tracey Watts Cirino is truly a class act. In this amazing book she shares her years of wisdom and experiences to inspire you to strive to become **Beyond Common**."

NeCole Cumberlander–Entrepreneur, Educator
and Motivational Speaker

BEYOND
COMMON

12 Essentials for Success in Life and in the Workplace

TRACEY WATTS CIRINO

emerge
publishing
TULSA, OKLAHOMA

25 24 23 22 21 20   8 7 6 5 4 3 2 1

Published by:
Emerge Publishing, LLC
9521B Riverside Parkway, Suite 243
Tulsa, Oklahoma 74137
Phone: 888.407.4447
www.EmergePublishing.com

Library of Congress Cataloging-in-Publication Data
ISBN: 978-1-949758-20-7 Hardcover
ISBN: 978-1-949758-65-8 Paperback
ISBN: 978-1-949758-21-4 Digital/E-book

BISAC Category:
BUS018000 BUSINESS & ECONOMICS / Customer Relations
BUS030000 BUSINESS & ECONOMICS / HR & Personnel Management
BUS066000 BUSINESS & ECONOMICS / Training

Printed in the United States

Table of Contents

Dedication

This book is dedicated to my husband, Anthony, for always believing in me even when I couldn't see it for myself. For always being my biggest cheerleader. For taking such good care of our two boys when I have been called to work endless hours in pursuit of our dreams.

Acknowledgments

No one ever creates anything truly meaningful alone. Everyone needs a positive team with supportive people by their side. I am truly grateful that I have been blessed with truly amazing people on my journey through this wonderful life.

First, I must thank my co-pilot on this great adventure, my husband, Anthony. You are the magic glue that holds everything together. You are my love and my light. Your love and support have made all the difference to me. Without you, I would not be the woman I am today.

I would like to thank my two wonderful children, Dominic & Christopher, who remind me every day what really matters most. You push me every day to be a better mother and a better person. My favorite part of every day is saying our prayers and what we are most grateful for together. I love you to the moon and back x infinity!

I am so grateful to my father for always believing in me and my dreams. For teaching me since I was young to stop and enjoy the ride, wind in your hair, to laugh, giggle and be silly even as an adult. Dad, I know you are smiling down.

My mom gets a huge thank you and a big hug for always cheering me on even when she was scared to death of what crazy dream I wanted to pursue next. Thank you for loving and supporting me every step of the way, especially the hard, challenging ones.

My stepfather, Mitchell, gets a huge thank you for teaching me that as a woman, I could do anything and that I could take care of myself and never be dependent on anyone or anything. You taught me your strong work ethic as you put pigtails in my hair and painted my nails as only a strong, confident man could do :-) xoxo

Thank you to my sister Jennifer for always being there for me no matter what and challenging me to grow outside of my comfort zone. I am grateful to have you as my sister and friend. I love you.

A very special thank you to my grandmother Natalie, who encouraged me to be fearless and courageous every day of her precious life. You were the first person to get me to really see the real me. I love you forever!

Thank you to my in-laws, Jack and Ginger. You have taught me so much about family and loyalty. I am grateful to you both for all you do every day to show up and support our family. I love you both so much!

As I said, no one achieves anything great alone. I would like to take this time to acknowledge all of the wonderful guests and supportive team members that have taught me so much and are the real reason this book is even possible. There are far too many to mention by name and I am truly grateful to each and every one of you. It has been your constant support and encouragement that has allowed us to grow and develop such a wonderful team.

Thank you to my dear friend and oftentimes second mother Rochelle. You have always helped me turn my wild ideas into words that people can actually understand. I am forever grateful for all your help, support and guidance all these years.

Thank you to Lora. You are not just a team member, but a true friend who has helped me grow as a leader and as a person. I appreciate every ounce of energy you pour into our team mission and vision.

Megan–thank you for all you do to help others and cheer on our team and for always encouraging me to delegate, delegate, delegate! Stacie–I love your wit and the charming way you told me you worked here by showing up to charity events before you even officially joined our team. Rachel–for always saying yes and your kindness toward putting our team first and confronting challenges even when it's uncomfortable. Caitlin–thank you for being the yin to my yang and being a true treasure that I have the honor and pleasure to work alongside. I love the way you get my dream and vision for our team and put it into action. Alicia - I am so grateful for all the help and encouragement you pour into me and our team daily. It has been an absolute gift that you have come into my life at the exact right moment.

I am super grateful to my Rusk family who has taught me that good enough is not really enough. I am forever grateful to you all for teaching me such wise leadership lessons all around the globe.

I would like to give a special shout out and thank you to my wonderful business coach and friend Sally Montavon from Summit Salon Business Systems and all the amazing wonderful people that are part of this extraordinary group of leaders, coaches and mentors. You all are such an extraordinary gift and I am forever grateful for you all.

I would like to give an extra special thank you to my group from *Goldman Sachs 10,000 Small Businesses Cleveland Cohort 13*. You all are an amazing treasure to me, and I am truly grateful to have you all in my corner.

Lastly, I need to thank my book publisher Christian and project manager Julie with Emerge Publishing. These two saw something special in this project before I really believed it could actually be a book. Their passion for believing in me and this project was beyond measure and I am forever grateful to have them on my team. Julie's commitment and dedication to seeing it through to the end is what true professionalism is all about.

Most of all, I would like to thank God. Thank you for picking me up when I fall down and showing me the way. Thank you for allowing your Holy Spirit to flow through me as I write this book. Your strength is the ultimate driver to keeping me on the path to live my best life and to connect with others in a *Beyond Common* way.

Foreword

I began my career in the medical science field, transitioned to financial management and have loved the last 35 years as an entrepreneur, mentor and public speaker in the professional salon industry. Life presents us with many interesting twists and turns which excite, challenge and at times scare us but ultimately make us who we are and lead us to a greater expression of ourselves and a more authentic journey through life. Today our company is designed with one single purpose, to empower salon and spa owners and salon professionals to earn a better living and live a better life!

This journey first led me to the author at a seminar I was conducting on leadership and communication in Florida some 15 years ago. Since that time, I have witnessed Tracey evolve from an inquisitive and sometimes frustrated seminar participant to a lifelong learner with the willingness to implement what she's learned and the courage to push through her own fears and insecurities. These qualities and her own life experience make her the perfect person to write a book focused on "Living Our Best Life."

I believe whatever our journey and wherever it takes us we all want to believe that what we do matters and that in some small way we can make a difference in this world. But let's not kid ourselves, we are immersed in a technological revolution that is disrupting and reengineering virtually every aspect of our life. Amid this massive change is the equally profound effect it's having on humanity as we spend more time every day interacting with the inanimate objects in our hands and less time interacting with other humans in a meaningful way. Our self-esteem is more closely connected to the number of likes we receive on Instagram from people we don't even know than it is to our own feelings of self-worth. Teenage anxiety and depression have reached an all-time high as we focus more on the things in life, we have no control over and less time perfecting the things we do. Things like our attitude, our communication, and how we present ourselves to the world each day. We have become obsessed with how others view us rather than how we see ourselves!

> **Beyond Common** *is a gem of a book that couldn't come at a more opportune time as a subtle and at times not so subtle reminder to all of us to "wake the F up," stop focusing on ourselves, lose the entitlement, stop worrying about the things we can't control and start focusing on the things we can!*

In a world increasingly influenced by technology it is imperative that we focus on being more human not less if we are to experience the true joy and fulfillment we seek. This is not a book for those who believe their destiny is in someone else's hands or for those who refuse to let go of their false beliefs and continue to blame, justify or deny their poor results. This is a book for those, regardless of their current circumstances, who desire to take full control and responsibility for their life and put into action the habits that will change their destiny.

In "Beyond Common" the author gives us an insightful look at what really matters and what allows us to make a human connection, a meaningful contribution to our lives and the lives of others by simply committing to become our authentic self. It's all about BEING! Being present, being nice, being a good listener, being and doing more than expected, being willing to learn new things, being kind to others, being loving and honest with ourselves and ultimately striving every day to be the best version of ourselves and live our best life.

Each chapter is rich with stories and practical examples from the author's authentic experience to help us see our blind spots, focus more on others, develop new habits and abandon old ones to become "Beyond Common" and ultimately enrich the quality of our life and the lives we serve.

This is a cause I can get passionately behind and so should you because everything you need to succeed is in these pages, completely within your control, and if you're willing to take the ride not even technology can disrupt your personal journey to being "Beyond Common."

Peter Mahoney

President
Summit Salon Business Center

Introduction

For the past 22 years, I have been extremely passionate about both professionalism and helping people reach their full potential. I have spent my entire life's work teaching, training, talking, asking questions, and listening to others' opinions on the wonderful, beautiful, often misunderstood subject of professionalism, which can be defined as competent, steady, thorough, dedicated and respectable (which sounds boring, right?). As far back as I can remember, I was infatuated with the idea of being all of these things. I know it's crazy, but more than anything, I love to talk with people and discuss ways they can level up their professionalism to how they take care of their customers, and how they can improve their personal development in and out of the workplace. It has been a passion project of mine for so long. You might think that it is a little weird to have a passion project based on professionalism, but I had an epiphany on the topic and I am just over the moon excited to share all of this with you! I just cannot wait for us to go on this journey together to learn and grow.

To me, professionalism is so important because it's our way of being present with people. It's our way of connecting the best we have to offer with other people in a bright and shiny way. Here's the thing, I love people. I love listening to people, connecting with them and, most of all, being kind and helping them.

I don't want to start off on a negative tone. But, I will do precisely that for the greater good of all who have suffered from a lack of professionalism or who have been a victim of the lack of reliability and dedication on the part of others. For some reason, it seems that nowadays, anything goes and there is a lack of professionalism. Is it infuriating to you when you walk into a restaurant, a doctor's office, a store or a school, for that matter, and people won't even look at you? Or don't even look up from their phone?

Why do people do this? Why has this become acceptable in society? Does this kind of behavior make you wonder, *What in the world is going on with people?*

Consider this analogy: During a recent hotel stay, a maid had her laundry cart and an extra-large rack of dirty towels blocking the entire hallway. All the while, I was standing there with my luggage, trying to check out with 14 other bags in my hand, and she was jibber-jabbering with her girlfriend. She did not care that the customer was struggling to get through and needed some assistance. As a hotel guest, I had not planned on standing there for 10 minutes—now that might be an exaggeration, but I'm pretty sure it was at least five minutes.

I know this wasn't intentional—she probably wasn't even aware. But if you are a working person, please pay attention. Be alert. Be awake. I just tipped you for cleaning my room, and now you are too busy talking to help me through the hallway.

Each of us has been in a similar situation. It happens every day. It doesn't matter where you are, where you're going or what you're doing. We each have dozens of stories about people who treated us badly or gave us poor customer service because they were not coming from a place of professionalism. It's not *if* this kind of thing happens, it's *when* and *how often*. I am the type of person who always wants to see the best in people and this type of behavior really makes me crazy because I want to see people at the top of their game and succeeding in life.

How do you expect to be the best in your field of choice in any industry you choose to go into? How do you become the best without consistently applying the traits of professionalism? Professionalism is the number one attribute that separates us from our competitors. If you have it, you stand out from the crowd and you will have your pick of any career you choose. You can work at the best companies with the best people. You will become *beyond common*!

As humans, it's about time that we level up and make this the norm. Wouldn't you rather go to places, work in places, shop at places and give your money to people who demonstrated or showed you somehow that they cared? The time has come and the time is now that we stop accepting bad behavior as a society norm and help people rise up to their true potential. This, my friends, is my mission and it is why I wrote this book. Every generation has people who are extremely successful and those who are not, and people who are lazy and people who think they are entitled to get paid the most for doing the least. I want to help people develop their full potential and it's really not that hard.

Life is about paying attention. Especially, paying attention to what's going on around you, what your customer's (or whomever you serve) needs are, what your children need, and what your boss needs. Also, this includes paying attention to the needs of your staff and also what your spouse and loved ones need.

The more we can operate from a place of professionalism, pay attention to each other and add value, the more we will feel the energy of connection to all other human beings. We are all seeking to feel special, loved, and connected. *Connection starts with waking up to professionalism.*

Who wouldn't want to wake up in a world where you are going to get a cup of coffee, and people actually look up at you, smile, and say, *"Good morning! How is your day going?"* Who doesn't want to go to a doctor's appointment and be spoken to as a real person with a life outside of the appointment? Wouldn't it be great if your doctor was able to see you on time for your appointment? Wouldn't you rather avoid the awkward over-sharing conversation with the young chatty salon stylist or similarly skip the whole nail salon "yelling at each other in a different language" routine? What if as a young person, your superiors talked to you with respect? Oh, and you responded to them with respect? Doesn't that sound like heaven to you?

No matter what your job is, do it with passion and heart. Have pride in your work and pour your heart into whatever it is that you are doing. Greatness only rises out of little things done thoughtfully and carefully. I often see great people working as janitors, taxi drivers or convenience store cashiers. When I ask them about their day, they are more than happy to share why they love their jobs with me. Almost always they say something about the joy they get from serving others.

We have to share this planet with others. Look up from your damn phone. Put a genuine smile on your face and say, "Hello, I am here for you! I get paid because of you–have you thought about that? Because it is true one way or another. We get paid at our jobs because of the people we serve–and I'm here to serve you in the very best way!"

Why read a book on professionalism or professional behavior?

I want to share with you my story. I went through a period of time as a stylist when I was broke, starving, living in poverty or close to, had my parents not let me live with them. I was completely clueless as to what it took to be successful. Contrary to what you may think or have thought in the past, there is no busy bus that pulls up with a load of people screaming your name who only want you because you showed up today and are ready for your life and career to begin. I am sorry if no one has told you the honest truth before. I am here to keep it real and tell you the truth! You will have to work for it and put your time in! *This is your life.* It is not a dress rehearsal and you do not get a participation trophy. You will be coached and cheered for along the way, but just showing up is not enough. You will get pushed and kicked in the gut and throat punched but either way, *you write your own life's story*!

So let's get back to the story. I started paying attention to all the people who appeared to be successful and were constantly busy. What were they doing that I wasn't doing? What was I missing? What were the next steps to success? I had gone to all the latest and greatest educational classes, and still, I was not getting ahead. If anything, I was starting to become entitled and whiny about not achieving what I wanted in life. I thought, *Well, I'm the best because I took this class and you didn't. I show up to everything! Where is my break?* Why can't the world see I am the best?

When I stopped to pay attention to what successful people were doing, I realized that they were taking personal responsibility for their lives and their actions. They weren't blaming the world for everything they didn't have. They were making things happen! They were being true professionals in every aspect of their lives and they were showing up for people in a beyond common way.

Now, you don't know me that well yet. But I hope by the end of this journey you will walk away knowing yourself better. *This journey is about you becoming the best version of yourself and you loving your whole self flaws and all.*

For everything I have ever accomplished, I always seemed to learn the hard way, taking the longest road with the most bumps and bruises. My wish is for you to start your journey towards professionalism much earlier on your path than my clueless ass did. I was never a quick study, so these things didn't happen overnight. They slowly became daily practices that developed into successful habits and that eventually led to success.

What if I told you that you could earn more money without changing careers, but instead, by working for the same company you currently work for? No matter what you do for a living, behaving like a true professional will always get you paid more for what you do. It will always get you picked first to head up a project or be a part of a group or organization you are passionate about. It will get you your dream job out of college or help you start your job when you finally figure out what you want to do with the rest of your life.

Even in the line at the grocery store, professionalism will get you better service, more smiles, and an all-around better view of the world. Now, I realize it's not always easy and you don't know what you don't know. This professional behavior does not always come easily to everyone. But if you put in a little effort on a consistent basis, I promise the rewards will pay you a great dividend and deliver you uncommon results.

What do you think the #1 complaint is from leaders, managers, and anyone in an executive or leadership position? I had my suspicion but I wasn't completely sure. For this reason, I started asking anyone who was willing to answer my questions and talk about their struggles. A principal of a well-respected private school said that for him, the dress code and staff not showing up on time for important meetings events, etc., were his biggest struggles. A hiring executive for a big bank, 130 small business owners, and just about any person who has ever held a leadership position has said that having the person who showed up for the interviews actually show up for work once they were hired was a major issue. Then I interviewed 250 young professionals ages 18-25 that were just entering the work force and guess what their biggest fear was? The fear of their boss finding out they had no idea what they were doing.

I thought, *Wow, these are three fairly easy things to do.* How do we inspire the people who are molding young minds to want to do it? After all, *Children are the future!* Well, here you go:

1. Dress for the job you want, not the one that you have.

2. Be early and prepared for important meetings.

3. Be yourself in your interview and truly represent and show up to work as you after that.

Do you want to know:

- How to stand out from the crowd and land your dream job or career?

- How to stand out from other companies and have your pick of top talent?

Everyone wants the career of their dreams, and everyone wants to be surrounded by the best employees. They want team members who get the culture and will 100 percent buy into your brand and company vision. We all want the same things but how do we expect to get them?

Do you do more than people expect? Do you bring more to the table than what you are paid to do? If not, then you have not done enough and that's okay, you just have some work to do. Keep going. Keep working until that is the norm for you. Only then will you be beyond common!

Now, I'd like to clarify and make sure I am sharing truly from the heart with complete transparency. I am not perfect at hitting 100 percent all of the time but I will get back up and try again even when I am scared and afraid. I am a lifelong learner who enjoys devoutly studying other people wherever I go. I am naturally curious about how we think, what we do, why we do it, and what we can improve on. I will

Beyond Common

forever be a work in progress and will always look for ways to grow and improve wherever I can, forever asking, "But, why?"

So, with that said, I profess myself ready to share and continue my work in this area for the betterment of all humankind! My life's purpose is to use my passion and creativity to inspire and motivate people in order to bring out the beauty in mankind as we open our hearts and share our compassion for all. I want you to succeed. I want you to live happily and for you to be respected by others and viewed as someone that stands out. I can help you and am so happy to do so! Now, let's begin the journey.

Who is this book for?

Anyone who wants to:

- Earn a *Beyond Common* income.
- Lead a *Beyond Common* team.
- Grow a company *Beyond* what is *Common*.

If any of these statements ring true to you, then this book is for you and I'm so excited to share it with you! It is my true passion to help people, and that is what has led me here to share these thoughts and ideas with you. If you use them and adapt them into your life as professional essentials, you will create and design the life of your dreams, and that will make you *Beyond Common*.

CHAPTER 1

Be Present!

- *Be present! Show respect! Be in the room!*
- *Be in the moment!*
- *Look up from your damn phone!*
- *Eye contact really. Please, look at me!*
- *Over here! I'm a real person.*
- *In case you didn't know, your phone is not a real person and you cannot phone-in being present.*

If you have ever wondered, *Why is this person not looking at me?* or, *Hello look, I'm over here?*, then this is the chapter for you!

In what universe would it ever be acceptable for people to look down at an inanimate object like a telephone instead of looking up at a human being who is right here before you? What makes this even crazier and a little insane is that in this day and age, service and technology should run hand-in-hand with helping one another.

People are choosing not to use technology for the greater good. Instead, they are constantly using it to ignore people who are right there in front of them. They are literally using technology to harm themselves and the people around them. I really have a problem with this when it comes to how we treat our families and our relationships.

Even more insane is when someone is being paid to do a job of any kind or if they have volunteered to do a job of any kind, but they are literally sitting there ignoring the people who they were hired to serve. This is the most infuriatingly crazy thing that has become a norm in our culture. As a society, we have started to accept this bad behavior and become numb to it. It's truly embarrassing. Why do we accept this?

If we take a moment to think about this, we wonder if anyone should get paid at all to behave like this? We can all agree that if you do not choose to do the job, why do you think you should get paid? We need to stand together on this one, especially women (after how hard we have worked for equal rights and to be taken seriously), and work together to raise the bar of professionalism. Gone are the days when we could ignore such poor behaviors on the job and sit back and watch society as a whole crumble and fall after how hard we worked as women to make a difference. And after working hard together to stand for something, I find this so infuriating. I know I'm not the only one out there who sees it this way or has experienced this type of bad behavior.

I talk to dozens, sometimes hundreds, of women on a weekly basis who are not happy about the lack of professionalism. If we can work hard to send a clear message that lets people know how important it is to put their best professional foot forward, we will have a stronger workforce. Also, we will be able to build highly productive teams that are rewarded and happy to thrive in their careers. We will have raving fans at small businesses across the country and the world over. If you will join me on this journey to raise the bar on professionalism for everyone and anyone who is in, or planning to be in, our workforce across the globe, or even if you do it for young people to inspire and motivate them that there is a better way, I know we can truly make a difference. If we do this intentionally, we empower each other and our teams to make a difference by being the most professional versions of ourselves possible.

Even if you are the type of person who wants to be comfortable, relaxed, friendly, and approachable, you can still be professional. Relaxed, friendly, and professional can work together. For a long time, people thought that *professional* had to be stuffy or rigid. I am not speaking about professionalism that is so rigid and stuffy that no one has any fun.

I am talking about professionalism that is conscientious, that adds value, that helps people feel welcome, that helps people feel wanted and included. Professionalism is about a state of inclusivity and bringing people together. Wouldn't that be an amazing thing if you felt wanted and appreciated by your co-workers, your team, where you shop, where you get your oil changed, your hair and nails done, or really any small business that you were choosing to do business with? This is the type of professionalism I'm speaking of. This is the type of professionalism that is attainable across the board if we start empowering young people to make a difference and be professional, to not be lazy and quit on themselves before they even get started so they can truly make a difference.

Show respect.

Is it okay to give your boss dirty looks and not so much as crack a smile when she says, "Hello," or "Good morning," to you? My immediate answer would be **NO.** It's not okay. It is never okay, and it *never* will be okay.

Why would any person, young or old, think that's acceptable? I'm not sure where this displaced temper tantrum comes from, but it is not okay. Here is a hot tip coming your way... I'm your boss, principal, team leader, mother, teacher or just a colleague. Maybe you will need to pretend to be a respectful person until you actually are. When a person sacrifices so much so that you can have a great place to work, learn, and grow, show a little appreciation. And maybe say, **"THANK YOU,"** once in a while, you ungrateful little troll. How many of you have felt like this before in one situation or another? Am I right?

What does respect mean to the average person? Respect yourself first, and then maybe it will be easier to respect everyone else. Treating people with respect should be as natural as breathing air. But somehow, some way, this has not been my experience when it comes to hiring and training people. Don't get me wrong. Lots of people surprise me all the time with how wonderful, respectful and kind they are, and I don't think there is one generation to blame over another. It all comes down to what someone has been taught about being respectful and having a good work ethic.

I am not afraid to be the person who shows others what that looks like and neither is anyone else on my team. We work hard to train on all of these life skills, not only the technical or business skills. It goes like this...You do dumb crap.

I will call you out on it again and again until you stop doing dumb shit! You, yourself, are <u>not</u> a dumb shit, you are actually brilliant and wonderful just as you are, and you simply need to be shown or told how to make better choices. I am never judging a person or a person's character, just adjusting some bad behavior and offering some other options.

Challenge the idea, not the person!

Never make yourself small for anyone. Never dim your light. "Shine bright like a diamond," as Rihanna says. ☺

Do the right thing
even if you think no one is watching.

Do the right thing even when you think no one is looking. It seems that someone is always looking or recording you on their iPhone. Being a professional person with integrity is about doing the right thing because it's the right thing to do. It's not for someone else to do. It's for you. Don't you want to live in a world where you can have absolute trust in the fact that someone washed the fork you are eating off of or the brush that they used to style your hair has been properly sanitized? Being a professional person that you can count on to do the right thing creates more of that kind of awesome energy for you everywhere you go. You get what you give, so please give the good stuff!

If you're not sure what to do, ask someone you respect. Don't ask someone who lacks integrity or a person you don't respect. If you want a good answer, ask a good person a good question. If you want excuses and bullshit, ask a person who lives their life filled with excuses and blame.

Only take advice from someone you would trade places with! Everyone else's opinion is BS.

If we all work together to be more professional and become better at how we treat each other, we can completely change the world for the better. The only thing standing in your way is the fear of not following the sleep-walking sheep into the world of ignorant bliss, worried too much about what others are thinking or just thinking of themselves.

I want to live in a world where everyone is putting their best foot forward, and we help each other to make progress and to become the best possible versions of ourselves. We all make mistakes but learn and grow from there.

I wish I would have learned this earlier in life. I say it to my team all the time. Don't worry about what others think of you. It is none of your business anyway! They are sleep walking and probably too worried about what others think of them or purely just thinking of themselves. Why should you care what they think or say about you? I ask people and myself, "What do you consider professional behavior?"

Here are some of the answers I get from time to time:

1. Arriving at work at least a half hour before your first scheduled appointment to plan your day: smiling, happy and ready to work.

2. On time is actually late.

3. Not talking about other team members or causing drama in the workplace. NO GOSSIP *Come on moms, stop teaching young ladies to gossip and cut down other women. This is why they think it's okay

and it becomes like adult bullying. WTF, wake up already and do better at teaching our children.

4. Ability to articulate a professional sounding email.

5. Ability to think for yourself.

6. Looking up at someone when you talk. Asking questions. Admitting when you have made a mistake early and getting others to help.

7. Using complete sentences and refraining from shouting out profanity in public or the workplace.

8. No whining.

9. Not expecting everyone else to do your job.

10. Treating peers, co-workers, owners, managers, and supervisors with respect.

11. Dressing for the job you want, not the one you have.

12. Showing up early for meetings.

Why do people say they want to change their lives and then don't follow through on their words with the right actions? What's missing? Having a business run smoothly and consistently is key. Making sure things are scheduled properly so people can work smarter instead of harder. Some people need a lot of hand-holding and simply want you to do it for them. Tell them the truth. They have to do it themselves. No matter how much we care for them, we cannot do it for them. I have learned this the hard way time and time again. I have fallen victim to wanting to believe the good in all will prevail by believing people's words when their actions don't align with what they say is important to them.

Look up from your damn phone while you are driving!

OMG! Seriously, you're driving a car. There are tons of people around. Don't you see it's dangerous to be texting while driving? I literally just saw this woman run her car onto a curb, almost take out an entire tree lawn, and she still did not look up from her phone while texting. Wow! That is really crazy. I am often so amazed by people's behavior! This woman definitely needed to be fully engaged in the task at hand. It's a blessing that no one got hurt and no one was run over.

If you are operating any type of machinery, it's a good idea not to be texting or doing other things. I am also amazed by the fact that students are able to text all day while in class. This does not seem like the best way to educate our youth. We would have much greater success if we withheld their phones while they're in class.

Now, don't get me wrong. Technology is a wonderful thing when used for good. I use my phone every day to take notes, to organize my life, set reminders, and all sorts of other useful things. But when used to rob us of our humanity, it seems much more like a weapon that can be misused to harm ourselves and others. When technology is used to communicate more effectively and to help level up what we once could not accomplish in weeks, but now we can do in a moment, that is so cool. We use it in the salon for digital consultations, for celebrating individuals and team victories. Please stop allowing technology to treat you like a **tool** and start using it only as the tool it is.

However, when you misuse technology in a harmful way, that is what I'm talking about. What if you would have hit and killed someone because you were texting and driving? Wouldn't that be a horrible burden to bear? Talk about tanking your self-esteem and self-confidence. You would be beating yourself up for the rest of your life because you took a human life simply by making that one horrible decision. We are all connected and live on this planet together. Our decisions matter and they affect others!

No text is worth a life or two because your life would not be the same the minute you had that pain hanging over you. Not to mention the family and loved ones who would lose someone because in a split second such a horrible decision was made. Now, I'm not naive enough to think that my preaching about this would make you change your mind. But if, for one second, we could all inspire each other to stop, take a breath, and ask ourselves, "Is this choice leading me to the best version of myself or is this choice helping anyone?" If you answer *no,* then don't do it. Do something else, anything else that leads to becoming the best version of yourself.

Questions for Reflection:

1. How do we connect in a real human way?
2. How do we connect with humanity while using technology for the tool that it is?
3. How can I stay present and pay attention to people?
4. What is more important to you—your phone or your family?

CHAPTER 2

Be Nice

Kindness always WINS!
Kindness is being honest even when it's hard!

So, what do you do when you are faced with options that are less than appealing? You have decided to be kind to everyone you know. Kindness always wins in the end. Why did I let that rude woman at the grocery store get the best of me?

It's like you are walking along thinking, *I'm a good person. I'm a really good person who wants to do good.* And *Boom!* I lose it when I'm faced with absolute rudeness by another human being lacking in any humanity or kindness for all I'm trying to do. Oops! Whose fault is it for my behavior? Well, it's absolutely mine, and I own it. And so should you!

I used to think—actually, not just think—I totally believed that the path to enlightenment was a destination. That one day, when I get there, I will be kind to everyone like all of those beautiful, kind, enlightened people I want to be like. When I get there, I will be so kind and just like them. Yay! They are so lucky! Lucky me! I have since realized this moment is what matters most. Just be kind in this moment. It's about the journey itself. It's not an end destination.

Back then, when I thought this way, I would get really mad at myself every time I made a wrong choice and got angry or mad at someone. I would think, *Oh, great! I'm not an enlightened person yet because I'm not good enough, this person got to me yet again.* Then, I would be really mad at myself and make all sorts of bad, unkind choices to punish myself and wind up feeling lousy.

Guess what? I probably wasn't that much fun to be around either. Beating on yourself for being human does not exactly set you up for being kind to everyone you meet. When I finally realized these life principles and that everything like it is a process, that is when I started to realize I had to be kind to myself first and love myself first! Wow! What a concept! Did I hear this golden gem correctly?

Yes! Be kind to yourself first! It's not selfish to be kind to **you**. When you treat yourself with kindness, you train others how to treat you. The first time I heard that was when I read Jack Canfield's *The Success Principles* book. I thought, *Whoa, this blows my mind,* because I had always thought that would mean you were selfish if you did anything for yourself first.

And it turns out, the only way you can be genuinely kind to others is by being genuine and kind to yourself. You matter, and the more you treat yourself accordingly, the more love you feel to give. Kindness is about giving. So, make sure you have it to give. As airline attendants say every time you take off on an airplane, make sure you get your mask on first. You know, you can't help anyone else if you can't breathe and you die first. Thus, it follows that you can't be kind to others unless you're kind to yourself first!

Did you know that sometimes being nice means being honest? Never ever think it's okay to say something just to hurt another person. But realize that if you are not honest with someone about what they are doing, you are not being kind. To be kind, you have to get over your need to be liked. So be kind enough to be honest and help the person in need who really needs to hear the truth.

When you are someone's team member, boss, coach, mentor or are in any kind of a leadership position, you must be kind and tell the truth no matter what. You are not helping anyone if you lie and tell them they are doing a good job when they are not performing at the level they need to perform. Sugar coating this, or diluting this message, will only cause you problems later. Trust me. I learned this the hard way several times.

I have a tendency as a fast-talking, kind of loud Sicilian woman to drop the hammer or come across as strong, direct, bold, intense or even aggressive. And in my efforts to soften this area of weakness, I would confuse my staff and dilute my message so much that I would get angry and frustrated when they didn't change or improve their behavior.

Now is it their fault? Absolutely not!

It's my fault, and I needed to figure out how to give feedback without diluting the content so much that no one knew what the heck I was trying to say. Another great example: "No, those are not pants if I can see your tush through them!" No matter what job you have, dress like the dream job you want, not the job you have. Whatever the most successful person in your chosen field dresses like at your dream job, dress like them!

Dressing for success is something you can control. Start off by dressing the way you feel the most confident. If you are the largest sized woman or the smallest sized woman in the room, it doesn't matter. When it comes to professionalism, leggings and tights are not pants. They never will be pants, and no one wants to see your tush. It makes everyone uncomfortable. Even if you have the best tush ever, cover it up with professional clothing. Please, for the love of God, invest in some actual pants to help yourself feel strong, confident, and put together. I mean this with absolute love and kindness and I love you enough to tell you the truth even if no one else will. No, those are not pants, and I can see your BUTT!

I will tell you if you have food in your teeth and a booger up your nose or you have lipstick all over your face or on your teeth. I will let you know that your fly is down and that you have a hole in the back of your pants. I will not tell you at the end of our conversation. I will not tell you after you walk off the stage unless that is the minute I noticed. Often times, I will say, "I love you and you are beautiful but you have something in your teeth!"

I did have to help a sister out that was on stage when I walked in before I was the next speaker. She was wearing a beautiful pink dress for her presentation, and while she was speaking, I noticed a hole in the back of her dress where her undies were peeking through. Now, I did not want her to feel embarrassed, but I wanted her to know. I quickly worked my way through the crowd so I could isolate her alone. I said, "Hi, great presentation. It's nice to meet you. You look beautiful, and I love your dress. I don't want to make you nervous or uncomfortable, but I want you to know that there is a hole in the back of your dress. What can I do to help you?"

She was so grateful and appreciated that I told her the truth, even when her friends did not. She gave me a giant-sized hug and us two female total strangers had a true sisterhood connection moment (you know that special moment when you get an extra long hug).

I said, "I told you the minute I noticed to spare you the embarrassment of wondering."

She replied, "Gee! I wonder how long I walked around like that?"

I said, "I really wouldn't worry about it. You look beautiful and gave a great presentation." Then, I gave her my sweater so she could walk off the stage with grace and dignity.

This is what real kindness and being nice to our fellow brothers and sisters looks like. Not being fake nice so you could laugh later at the expense of someone else. "I would rather laugh with you than at you," and that is why true kindness always wins. In fact, I just recently witnessed a group of girls staring at a friend who had a tag hanging out of the back of her dress. They did nothing to help her. To me, these are not true friends and I would think twice about spending time with people who don't have your back. If they are not honest with you about the little things, then they cannot be trusted to be kind enough to be honest about the big, really important things. Wouldn't it be great if we could have more people around that we could trust to be honest and kind? What a wonderful world this would be!

Sometimes, you have to allow yourself to feel it! Don't run away or get a big head about it. You need to feel things to teach yourself that nothing will hurt you more than the stories you make up in your own head. Allow yourself to feel hurt, angry, sad, excited, happy, and on top of the world. But, remember these are just moments and they too shall pass. You are never too good to learn more and there is no shame in starting over.

Life is about living, and that includes a full range of all of our **human emotions**. We all naturally seek pleasure and avoid pain. But what we view and feel as being joyful or painful is what makes us all so different. We are all connected in the way that we feel things. And all human beings seek to belong and have our emotional needs met.

One of the major issues we face right now, as a society, is our obsession with not wanting to feel anything at all. Most people try to numb out completely and feel nothing and that is a real problem facing us today. Right? If you don't like something, you find a way to numb it or push it away.

There is currently an opiate epidemic in this country. People from a wide range of economic means and generational ranges are struggling with an addiction to feel nothing. Pain pills and other various drugs take away the pain and lead us down a path to seek out feeling nothing and numb-out all of the pain life gives us. My personal belief is that this is not just an opiate epidemic or some type of crazy drug epidemic that is killing thousands and thousands of people. This has affected everyone I know from all walks of life in some way. The statistics are frightening. I believe the root cause is a self-esteem issue. If there is one problem, issue or disease I wish I could cure for every human being it would be to end the burden of low and no self-esteem. This one thing could be the answer to cure so many. If no one has told you yet today, I love you and you matter!

We cannot outrun our DNA.

We are human, with real human emotions that sometimes are messy, but all the time, we have irrational human emotions. It's better to know what we feel and why we feel this way than to try to outrun our human genetic ways. We can all agree that we are seeing the negative side of this play out in the world today.

We are all connected in the way that we feel things. All human beings seek to belong no matter what false persona we put up. No matter what false persona we put up. We all have a need to feel love and need to feel a part of something bigger than ourselves! As long as we set our intentions to help, not hurt others, telling the truth is one of the best ways to be kind to others.

Asking yourself how it feels to be a true professional and be treated like a true professional is a really good way to get started. Self-discovery is what it's all about. If you're not sure how it feels, then ask yourself what it looks like to be a professional. Ask, "What do I see the most professional people that I respect doing?" Being professional is about valuing people, and if we can all level up our game and do this a little bit better, the world will be a kinder and better place for all of us to live out the lives we've dreamed about.

Are you with me? This kindness business is not for wimps. When we think of kindness, we may think of rainbows, sunshine, and moonbeams, but we realize true kindness takes heart and grit to truly live it and deliver.

Questions for Reflection:

1. How do you show kindness to people?

2. What is your definition of kindness?

CHAPTER 3
Listen

This is how you will solve problems and help people, right?

When you get together with people, are you genuinely interested in what they have to say? If you are, then you are on your way to becoming *BEYOND COMMON* and, in my opinion, an all-around wonderful human. If not, that's okay. It's time to get interested because you've got some work to do.

When you truly listen to others without worrying about what you are going to say next, you are going to connect with people in a really profound way. This will help you help others. The more people we help, the more people they will help and then so on and so on. We will be living in a caring professional world that we can be proud of. We are all connected, so listen with intention and get connected.

Listen to what people are trying to tell you. Ask questions. Repeat it back to them to make sure you got it right and that is what they were trying to say. We can all learn from and help each other at any given time. You never know what is going on with people, so ask questions and get interested. Get to know them in a way that lets them know you genuinely care about them.

Remember them. How is everything going? Is your mom feeling better? How was your vacation? What is new with you? Who do you love? Who do you respect? What have you done lately that really excites you? What moves you? What is the funniest thing you have seen or heard lately? Have you learned anything new lately? What are you reading?

Spend more time listening than talking. Oftentimes, we work so hard to make sure we look good to people or that people will know that we know what we are talking about. This makes us forget to make sure the other person feels good. It's not about you. It's about who you are serving.

This comes up all the time when I am coaching and mentoring young people or business owners. They are often so afraid of feeling insecure and about not knowing something that they overcompensate by not listening. Or they say yes to something they have no intention of doing or don't know how to do. They spend so much of their energy trying to impress people that they miss the real opportunity to connect with people. I am personally guilty as charged here.

It is so common that most people are unaware they are doing it. So when you try to point it out to them, they get defensive and say they know. I always listen. Previously, I would never do that. Oh, but you hardly do any listening and that is exactly what's holding you back from living the life of your dreams. I simply ask a person I'm coaching, "Are you getting the results you want? Making the money you want? Having meaningful relationships?" If they say, "No, I'm getting these results but I really want this," I will next ask, "Do you see a gap between what you do want and what you are currently getting?"

Results don't lie. If there is a gap, then changes need to be made in your listening style. If I say, "How are the results you are getting?" and they say, "*great,*" I say, "*God bless.*" If you are happy, then keep doing what you are doing. If you are not getting the results you want, then it's time to change something. You cannot do the same things over and over and think you are going to get a different result. That is the definition of insanity.

I hope you and I are getting to know each other better and the reason that I am able to speak so bluntly and say all of this is because I have done this numerous times. I have been so stubborn and pigheaded that I did not hear what people were saying to me. I speak freely about this topic because it takes me 12,000 times longer than everyone else to learn anything. Moral... you can still become an expert if you fail enough.

Do you know the most successful people have failed more than anyone else? I like to think about my biggest failures being more like my greatest opportunities to learn. I kept trying to impress people by what I knew, and I was saying, "Hey, look at me. I'm really educated. I'm really worthy. I did all the training. I am an educator. I'm a platform artist. I am a salon owner. I am this, I am that. You know I got this award and I have taken this class and I have the certification to prove it. Look at me!"

At the end of the day, people do not care why you have done what you have done or what you really know. Or for that matter, people don't care if you know anything at all. They care about you making them feel special. They care about feeling like they're important, special; maybe the most important person in the room. So when I am listening and getting to know someone, I really focus on what they need from me. I ask myself, *How can I serve them? What can I do to make their day? What's going to really help them to feel special, important, even loved? What if this is the best moment of their week? How can I really make it count?*

We sometimes need to feel heard and that is all the connection we need. I find all the time that the number one reason a client wants to change who they go to within the salon is because things got stale. They don't hear me anymore. They don't offer change, anymore. They take me for granted. They weren't listening to what I really needed. They were simply deciding for me without letting me know why. They didn't offer change and it made me feel like they didn't care and that I was insignificant. Does this sound familiar to many of the relationships we all have? Whatever the relationship—spouse, significant other, friend, sister, brother, mother, father, boss, etc.—we have all suffered from feeling less than in many of our relationships.

Now, I never want someone to feel neglected or not taken care of. So, I might overdo it and say some crazy stuff like, "Let me offer you this big change or something over the top," so that they know I'm the person who they need to be with for the change. Now some people feel great just getting the same thing again and again and that is awesome because I'm still listening to them. I am still providing the best service possible to make sure all their needs are really being met. I want them to know they matter to me!

You might be sitting there saying, "Wow! I am not listening or giving people my attention. I've had that feeling where I didn't even realize I was not listening to people at all." Don't worry. I've been there too and I want to help and share my secrets to help you. It takes practice. It takes dedication. It's going to take you staying conscious and awake and alert, but the first step is acknowledging you could do better when it comes to listening.

The rest of the world is walking around closed-minded and most of them think they're the best listeners in the world. They think they are perfect at everything, even though they're not getting the results they want. They think it's everybody else's fault. They blame it on the world and don't realize that if they could spend a little more time listening, making others feel special and important, they could be the best version of themselves.

I *truly* love helping people. And I love helping people see themselves in a different light. Finding a way to let their true inner beauty shine outwardly is really what lights my fire. I love being able to design a look that allows people to see themselves in a different way. I love helping new young service providers in our salon or new business owners—and our newest members of the hairdressing community—find their ability and their voice to do this for others. It is truly the most exhilarating and fulfilling moment. I love seeing the look on their face when everything clicks and you know they got it! All the kicks in the gut and teeth. This is the moment that makes everything worth it for me! It totally lights me up!

This all only happens by truly listening to what people need to help them solve their problems and see themselves in a different way than they ever have before. It doesn't matter what you do for a living, or what you're trying to achieve, as long as you spend more time listening and helping people solve their problems. The more you do this for others, the more your dreams come true. Give them the opportunity to look good in any way you can.

I didn't say, "Fix people's problems." I said, "**Listen**, when given a chance." That is how you're going to earn the respect of so many others now and again and again. Don't get me wrong. I know it sounds so simple and I know this is really hard. I'm not claiming that anyone can achieve perfection. I know that I work on this every day! It is not a **Set it** and **Forget it** kind of activity. Even though I totally wish it was the case for you and for me! I think I may have even thought it was done once I figured it out the first time. LOL!

It's a lifelong journey to listen, be present, and be a part of the conversation in a way that helps as many people as possible.

And no, I'm not talking about the kind of listening in which you simply nod and say, "uh-huh," the kind of *I do not care* type of listening that some husbands are guilty of. I mean, even sometimes wives are guilty as well. We all do it. I'm talking about the kind of listening in which you're really listening to their every word. You're not listening simply because you're waiting for your moment to talk. You're reading their body language or taking it in. You're reframing what you just heard them say. You are paraphrasing and saying things back to them that you heard them say.

You are not simply hearing one thing and running with it. You're repeating it back to them and giving them the opportunity to tell you if that's what they meant to say. In a kind way, you repeat, "Is this what you said? Is this what you meant?" Do not be mad or frustrated. Give people the chance to speak and the space to say what they really mean.

Make every little effort to stay engaged and involved in the conversation to ensure that you are truly listening—to hear the other person rather than find a moment that you can interject with what you think you know better. Sometimes, people don't want to fix it or figure it out. They just want to chat and feel like they've been heard.

I'm the type of person who really enjoys making others feel good about themselves. Remember to be a great listener and utilize the skills of active listening earlier in your life so that you dedicate time and develop the practice of active listening. I promise you the easier it gets, the better and more fulfilled life you will lead. This is one of those amazing practices that I most truly wish I had been taught at a younger age. This is such a profound thing and this is why I am so excited to share it with you. Something as simple as listening can change the course of your life. I wish there was a guidebook like this when I was young, or there was someone who was willing to speak to me honestly, truly, and sincerely. Here's the skill—if you work on it, your life will be better. Don't just do it sometimes. Do it daily like brushing and flossing. I truly believe that something as simple as listening better with more concentration and being more present will only improve your life. It's a rather small deposit with a big return. Full disclosure - I totally have bright and shiny object syndrome and if I can do it then so can you!

Sometimes, listening involves what they call active listening, which means listening not with the intent to go next with what's on your mind but to really listen in a way that gives the other person complete control of which direction the conversation is heading. Another thing to remember is not to talk too much. Give the other person the space to answer your questions. Do not answer for them.

When I work with guests in the salon or train new service providers, team members or coaches, I always listen. I listen deeply with the intention to understand what they are saying. I ask lots of questions and I listen to their responses. Now, don't get me wrong. I love to talk and have great, deep, meaningful conversations about hopes, dreams, and visions of what is possible to really get me going. I could completely lose track of time when I am in a real heart-to-heart connected conversation. But I am not perfect at this listening thing. I will forever be a work in progress because I love to talk and move fast, and I usually see things that others may not.

Listening is the magic that will help you give people what they want and need and that is what being *Beyond Common* is all about. Getting over yourself and your own agenda about what you want and really listening to others is the key to building great relationships. I am so very blessed to have served so many people over the years in this way.

I love it when someone tells me they have always had bad hair, or do not know how or what to do with it, and I am able to show them that they really do have good hair by asking the right questions and listening. When we listen intently to people and then respond with an answer that can help them, this is where absolute connection magic happens. This is what I love best about serving others. It also makes me the type of professional that people really enjoy working with.

If I can show you how to look and feel better by simply changing a few things, would that make you happy? If I could show you some tips and techniques that would save you time getting ready every morning, would that be of value to you? Based on listening and response, I respond accordingly and start to foster trust in our relationship.

One of the areas where listening is so important is when you are dealing with customers. People want to be heard and feel like you understand them. They do not want to hear about your system or your company policies or any of your whining for that matter. When you are helping serve people in your job, remember that they are why you are here. Whether directly or indirectly, everything you do in your job is because of the customers or people you serve. Customers are why we get paid and pretty much serve as our bosses.

If you only take away one positive attribute from this book, listening is that most important attribute. In most of these cases when dealing with customers, you must remember to listen with the intent of understanding where they are coming from, and then make them feel understood and appreciated for their feedback.

Do not go into it expecting to be **understood**. This sounds so simple, which it is, but doing something this simple is not always easy. Sometimes, it's hard. It took me years to get this one but once I did, I thought, *Aha, Aha, I get it.* Wow! Was I living in a world of misunderstanding before that? It was one of my mentors, John C. Maxwell, who says in several of his books and teachings. "Seek to understand, not to be understood!" The only way to achieve this is to listen attentively to another human being. This is where all understanding happens.

Because I spend so much time on this in my own personal development and in developing people in my companies, I get really frustrated when I am out in the world being a customer or just a human and people do not listen. I observe it happening all the time. And I think, *Oh wait! If you would simply stop talking and instead focus on listening, you could fix this right here so quickly. Please stop talking and listen to what this customer right in front of you is saying.*

It also happens to me when I am dealing with all the necessary operational specifics that it takes to run my business. I want to know why so many people who deal with people in their job or chosen profession do not listen when that is what they are paid to do.

If you are wondering how listening can help you to excel in your career, or help you win people over if you are at a different stage of life, listen up. When you listen, you can help solve people's problems. I have a real simple formula for this when coaching, parenting, training or selling:

- Listen for the problem.
- Identify the problem
- Offer a solution or a few possible solutions.
- Use a testimonial backed by facts.

Questions for Reflection

1. Who do you look up to?
2. Do you let them know?
3. What do you value most?

CHAPTER 4

Be More–
Do More than Expected

Be all in
Be loyal
Do what you say you will do!
Do more than expected
Be more than you ever dreamed.

I f you learn and use the techniques I am about to show you, you'll avoid getting downsized. Or, for that matter, you'll avoid being let go from any team, company or organization. And if you learn the techniques and make them your own by using them, you'll get picked first by every company you interview at. If you are the one conducting the interviews, then you will get happy, passionate employees who are truly loyal and will take excellent care of your customers. Here are a few interesting strategies that will help you earn an above average income and get gratifying, rewarding work.

Simply because everyone else walked by the piece of trash on the floor doesn't mean you should too. Understand that you need to be more, and do more than expected. If you think that things need to be better no matter where you are, where you live, and what you think you have or don't have to offer, you can do more. Each and every one of us has the ability to do more. This one really resonates with me so **much** because for such a big part of my life, I played the victim and didn't even know it.

I thought that the world owed me something if I showed up. And since I was the best at it, I thought people should treat me like I'm the best. That's when I thought I added value, and oh boy, did I ever have it wrong, so terribly wrong. If you notice that something needs to get done, you should do it. If you have the time and energy to complain about it or think that someone else should do it, then you have the time to be the one to do it.

A true leader will notice what needs to get done. Even if you don't notice, ask someone what else you could do and what else needs to be done. Another great thing to ask is: what are you working on that I could help with? It doesn't matter if this is at work or college, if you work for a non-profit, are helping your family take care of a sick parent, or if it's just in your own family—your own children, spouse or siblings. Anywhere in life, you can ask, "What are you working on? Can I help?" And people everywhere will appreciate it and will appreciate you! As a female leader, this is truly something I appreciate more than anything else.

People will absolutely love you for this. You will be the type of person who people want to be around because they know they can count on you. And let's face it. Isn't that what we all truly want? We want to be loved and appreciated. We want to have great meaningful relationships. We want to be connected to others. The way to do this for others and yourself is to do more. Do more from a place of love and understanding!

Now, you can't do more for others unless you are well taken care of. You must take care of yourself and do things every day that make you feel good. Make certain your actions are in line with your hopes and dreams. If there is a job or promotion you want, an invention you want to create, or a man or woman you want to marry, you must get out and do more. Do more of the things that fill your heart with joy! Do more of the things that a person who has the job you want, or a person who has a great invention, would be doing. You need to get out and take action. So get out there and do something that *moves you*. Do something that makes you happy every day! Try new things. Love yourself. Help yourself feel great, so you can go out and create change by helping others.

Have you ever wondered why you got passed over for a promotion, why friends didn't invite you to go to something that you wish they had, or you have just felt left out? Chances are you are not demonstrating the type of behavior that is showing others that you are all in.

When you are **all in**, people want to be around you. People enjoy doing stuff for you. They love being with you. When you want to be a part of something larger than yourself, you will magnetically attract people with the right energy into your life who you want to be around. So it doesn't have to be something big. But start today doing more than you did yesterday and you will see a positive shift in your happiness in as little as 30 days.

Make a list of all the tasks a person who had your dream job would do and start doing them. If you already have your dream job, show appreciation and gratitude, make a list of all the ways that you can improve or put some of your personal joy into tasks that you absolutely love to do into it. Start doing the type of tasks that you love daily.

Do the right thing even if you think no one is watching.

What do you want to be known for?

What would you like people to say at your funeral? I know this sounds a little morbid to some people, but we don't face this reality enough. You cannot change this. It is a part of life. Everything alive eventually dies one day. This is no big surprise. So why not accept this and think about what you would like to be known for? What do you want people to say at your funeral? Live like there is no tomorrow! What will make you feel like you had a life well-lived? This is not a mystery. This is #truth!

If you see people going through some of life's struggles like a divorce, unemployment or loss of a loved one, think about what would be helpful to you if you were in their shoes. What would you need? What would be some things that may help them breathe a little easier during a trying time? Use your *common sense* to understand what other people might need.

Oh wait, sense is not common! I repeat, sense is not common! I know this will shock most of you because we all go around telling stories about this and that and we say things like, "You know, just use your common sense."

I am the only one who has been guilty of judging someone on his or her lack of common sense. Well, that's okay. I own that now. I discovered years ago that sense is not common. No matter where you come from or what you think, it is common or normal for somebody else to think something completely different from you. And that is common and normal. Therefore, sense is not common and that is okay. You can work with this as long as you know it and own it. I hope you never forget sense is not common! Since learning about sense not being common, we train people in our company on "this is how we do it here" even when it's some little thing that someone else would say, "OH, it's just common sense." Knowing sense is not common sets you free from thinking others should know what you are thinking.

If you want something done a particular way, you need to show people exactly how you want it done and then let them do it. Stand right next to them. And be there to help if they need it, but let them do it. Give them some feedback, but let them do it. After they have done it well a few times, move away from them. And as they continue to do it, keep moving further and further away from them until they don't need you to be there to make sure they do it right. They can do it right all on their own.

I like to call this **See Do Go Know.**

- Show me so that I can **see**.
- Let me **do** it so that I can feel.
- Let me **go** so that I can **know**.

Allowing people the space to make mistakes and figure things out for themselves will allow them to develop their thinking muscle and alleviate so much of today's anxieties. Some people have never been given the opportunity in their life to think for themselves. Everything has been done, thought out, and planned for them. Hence, they do not know how to think or do not have any sense of what common sense might look like. If this is where someone is, you have to meet them where they are.

If you are the trainer, you cannot train them from where you are. You must train them from where they are. This is still a challenge for me because I still think everyone who knows me is living in my brain with me. Don't you? So, I definitely struggle here. But I am getting better every day at meeting people where they are with no judgment because I know sense is not common and what may be common sense to me might be absolute crazy talk to someone else. Or someone who is an actual rocket scientist might think what he is doing day to day is common sense and we would probably look at him as if he were the crazy one because there is nothing about anything you said about that rocket science that is common sense to me.

Knowing that we must dig deeper to connect with people in a real human way simply allows us to realize that as much as we are all connected, we are all different because of all of our own experiences that have brought us each to this exact moment in time with our own unique sense of conditional beliefs and how we view the world. I like to think of this as the different colored glasses that we view the world with. What color are your glasses? On the other hand, if you are the one who realizes that you need to step it up and get some sense about you and what you are doing, then you are in luck because knowing that you need to step it up is the hardest part. Yay! Hooray! You are making progress and I am so proud of you.

"Day sleeping" is what many people do. It is when people go through life asleep and never pay attention to what is happening around them. You might be awake and look fully functioning and completely normal to anyone walking by, but you are completely asleep at the wheel of life. So if you know you need to gain or get some sense to wake up or radically shake things up, you are in luck. Because if you go beyond common and finish reading this book and apply what you are learning, you will get some sense! Just follow these seven steps to get to *Beyond Common* results.

Step 1: Know that you need it.
Step 2: Surround yourself with people who have it and don't allow those that don't share those qualities to bring you down.
Step 3: Ask them if you could shadow them or if they will mentor you.
Step 4: Apply what you see.
Step 5: Ask for feedback and make any changes that need to be made. Learn from mistakes.
Step 6: Celebrate your progress.
Step 7: Repeat.

These are all simple steps that will give you big results. However, like I always say, simple doesn't always mean easy. The more you put these steps into practice, the easier it will be to be *Beyond Common*.

The challenge most of us run into is that most people don't know that they have no sense and they don't ask for help, because they are afraid and insecure about what they don't know. They think that if they just fake their way through life, others won't notice. Knowing that you will stand out from 90 percent of the people in the world just because you care enough to better yourself by reading a book like this makes me truly happy because we as a people are growing closer in connection and maybe we can help each other gain some actual sense. ☺

Always know what is required and expected of you to complete a job or fulfill a task. Have clear communication on both ends. What is required? What do I need to contribute?

Be persistent. This is the only way to achieve more than what is expected and gets you on the path to becoming the best version of yourself!

Do what you say and say what you do!!

Own your own choices and decisions. If you say you are committed to a cause, a person, a job, and a career, be real and do what you say you are going to do. When people are counting on you, speak up in a respectful way if you are not happy about something. Flipping out and doing things on an emotional whim makes you look inconsiderate like a snake in the grass.

Ask yourself, "What can I learn from this situation? What role did I play in creating this current situation?"

Trust no one. No, just kidding. For a moment, though, it will feel that way. You can tell a lot about others by their actions. They may talk a good game but their actions say something completely different! Trust your instincts and question bad behavior when you see it. Or any strange behavior for that matter! Do not accept bad behavior of any kind. You are worth so much more!

I used to be naive and believe that whatever someone said they would do, they would really do it. Now, I have learned that when we say we want this and that, or if we say we are going to do this or that, a person's actions must match up with their words. Observing behavior to match up with what is coming out of one's mouth is huge! I have learned over the years not to give my time and attention to those whose words and actions do not align. If you are putting in a 5 on the effort or willingness scale, I will no longer show up for you at a 10. I learned this from my coach and mentor Sally Montavon, who never stops amazing me with her golden nuggets of wisdom.

If you are the one whose words and actions do not align, stop and take the time to figure out why. Ask yourself what it would take for you to show up as a 10 in this area of words and actions aligning.

Service to others is the price we pay for the space we occupy. I want my life to be a miracle and to inspire other miracle lives. Figure out what you excel in and go out into the world and do it! Go out and do good.

How do we create a customer experience that feels like a first kiss? Something truly memorable? If you can go above and beyond what is expected or what is the norm, that is what will be memorable. Remember, we live in the experience age. The information age is dead. People remember experiences and how we made them feel. Anytime you can add a sensory touch to your customer experience, the more memorable it will be because the power of touch and connection go hand in hand and make everything that much more memorable like a first kiss.

Be the person who remembers all the important special holidays and life events. These dates are so important to people as they make them feel special. Celebrate them. Life is not easy most of the time so celebrate things that matter to people! Don't you think that is memorable to most people?

Questions for Reflection:

1. What do you want them to say at your funeral?

2. What do you need to become the best version of yourself?

Success Scale of Life

- No matter where you are, it's about helping you figure out where you are and where you want to go?

- Always be creating a culture of happiness wherever you go. Am I helping people live their best life?

- Do your words, actions, behaviors, clothes, makeup and all say that you are living your best life? Do they say you are happy and you are here?

CHAPTER 5

Practice on Your Time!
Learn on Your Time! ☺

I f you are trying to polish and perfect your craft, whose
time do you practice on? Not your client who is paying for
your time. Practice on your time!

If you can find a way to get paid to play, by all means
do it. That will set you up for great success on your professionalism journey. But do not practice on your client's time.
They are paying for your expertise and your skills. No matter what level you are at, be willing to put in the time and
practice so that you can learn and grow to become the best in
your field. It takes 10,000 hours of perfect practice to master and perfect your craft—not five minutes and then giving
up. What are you committed to doing for 10,000 hours?

If you cut someone's bangs too short because you were
not fully engaged or you were trying out something for the
first time, is that very professional? The answer is **no**! If you
do not know exactly how much to cut, put down the scissors
and practice on mannequins, your family, or your friends
until you get it right. I have never met anyone who appreci-

ated a stylist doing their first haircut on them. Never, ever, anywhere!

Once you get it right, do it 20 more times to make sure you have ironed out all the kinks. Your clients will appreciate that you treat them with respect and professionalism. This will create a lasting impression with your clients and they will rave about you to all of their friends on Instagram and Facebook, and even strangers whom they run into at the grocery store. People love to let people know when they have the best experience whether it's a salon, restaurant, wedding planner, accountant, photographer, doctor, new book (hint, hint), etc. They can even give you a 5-star review on Google or Yelp. Please let them brag about you a little.

One of my biggest pet peeves is to see someone on their personal phone. No matter what environment—a doctor's office, car repair service center, department store or salon—your number one priority is your patient, customer, or client. It drives me absolutely crazy when I see someone on their personal phone when they are at work. Another point, if you are on the phone for work and someone walks in, politely cover the phone and whisper to them, "I will be right with you." People need to be acknowledged. In other words, pay attention and put down your damn phone!

Do you see this happening everywhere you go? I mean, I've been in line at the grocery store with five to ten people waiting and the person who's supposed to be checking us out is on her phone. I have no idea what she's doing. But being on her phone doesn't feel like what she was paid to do. I wish someone would speak up and let this employee know that this is not acceptable behavior in any way, shape or form.

You are not adding to this customer experience. You are not helping and you're getting paid to do what exactly? If you are getting paid, why are you not working? The fundamental root cause of this whole issue is that for some reason, people think they don't have to be working. But you're getting paid, so you should be working. I don't think there's another option here. It doesn't matter what you're making per hour or how you get paid. That is not what I'm talking about. If you are working or at work, there is a certain standard you must meet. It is non-negotiable. If you are at work, then work. Customers are the basis of businesses and they must be served with excellence. It is not okay to ignore a customer or do a lousy job at serving them. Treat the customer as if they are paying your paycheck because guess what, they are! They are all our bosses.

Go talk to a customer but don't talk to your friends. If you are working, then work. And if you think there's nothing to do at work, find something to do. There seems to be a thought process in the world right now that allows people to think that they are the most important thing and they don't have to take initiative. They feel that they don't have to do everything because someone else will do it or it's not their responsibility because nobody taught them. Well, I have news for you. It's time to look beyond yourself and understand that if you want to get better at anything, you need to be practicing on your time and learning on your own time. If you're working, focus on your work and becoming better at what you do.

If your boss reached in and pulled $10, $20, $30, $40, or even $100 out of your purse or your pocket, that would be stealing, right? My belief is if you are not working and you're on company time, then it's the same thing as stealing. You wouldn't ever want somebody to reach into your wallet or purse and take money out! Wouldn't you consider that stealing?

Would you pay someone any money if they were not working? Every time I have asked this question to anyone that worked with me they always say, "Ahh, I get it now! No, I would not pay you if you were not working." Okay, then why should you get paid for not working? This is the same thing and I'm being honest. I've felt like this my whole life, long before I owned my own business. Therefore, this is not just because of being on the other side of the fence. I felt the same way when I would see others taking advantage of my boss. I would say, "Hey, what are you working on?"

I am all for having fun and making sure that you enjoy your work. Even get your customers involved in the fun. I think it's important to have a good time with your co-workers and enjoy working together to accomplish one common goal. It's not the working part that I see as an issue. These things are just like the fundamentals of life. Putting joy into our work is really the best.

I know it feels like I'm preaching at you and that is because I really want to help you understand and to learn all of this so that you are viewed as someone with a good work ethic and a person with integrity. Sometimes, this kind of knowledge doesn't come naturally to people and that's OK. In order to shine and become the best version of yourself, you need to learn how to do that. If you want to be able to land an amazing job, have a fulfilling career, be supported by others and be a person that someone wants to work with, you need to practice putting others first. That's what this book is for!

These days, if you want to stand out and become the absolute best version of yourself, be able to land an amazing career, have people always want you back and want to work with you and be a part of your team, this is the kind of stuff you need to realize. Putting your best self forward involves you learning on your own time. Got it? If you want to better yourself and your career and work, you have to practice on your own time. That is the only way to truly move ahead. This is not a Tracey Rule. This is a life-skill rule. ☺

Another thing that has become absolutely mind blowing as far as I have observed is sometimes, it's our parents who want to talk to us or text us all day while we are working. That's not exactly acceptable either. Sometimes, you have to sit with your parent/parents and let them know it's time to cut the cord and allow you to be an independent adult who needs to thrive and flourish. Also, tell them you need to be 100 percent on it while you're at work. And after you leave work, then you have the time to visit with family and friends. Do you hear? If we are 100 percent focused on our work when we are there instead of social stuff, then we would be more efficient. Then, when we do leave work, we can be 100 percent focused on taking care of ourselves and doing stuff that we love and enjoy. So, let's fill ourselves up with joy and feel good about ourselves and our relationships.

In most instances, people start at an entry-level job. Entry level is going to ensure that you learn the ins and outs of the profession so that you give yourself the time to develop and grow. You pay attention and learn from your mistakes. And entry-level positions are where you can learn a lot, observe a lot, and grow a lot, as long as you're paying attention. But if you don't pay attention and learn what you don't know, you are not ever going to get further ahead; this becomes a problem. A seed has to grow into a flower. You can't skip the part where the seed is planted, watered and nourished. IT TAKES WANTING TO BE SOMETHING MORE TO ACCOMPLISH IT. The time of growing and nourishing the seed is just as important as being the beautiful flower! You cannot skip this just because you want to be the beautiful flower today.

Oftentimes, our parents forget this and they are the ones who are interrupting us while we are trying to work and become young responsible adults, growing to have our own mind, our own independence, and even our own money. So, at your entry-level job, it might not seem like much and they might think you deserve more. And honey, you probably do, but everyone has to start somewhere. We all have to start somewhere and grow from there. There's a lot of learning to do — both personal and professional. And technically, that needs to happen in most careers and industries and this is your time to do that. Without these entry-level positions, we're going to pay top dollar to people who have not developed the skills, muscle, talent, or know-how. Now seriously, who would do that?

I've had to teach and coach people to perform at a high level because most people don't know how to perform at a high level right out of the gate. It takes time and attention to detail to perform in any career at the highest levels. Getting paid more is going to make the problem worse. Therefore, I do not believe in throwing money at people who don't possess the skills that they need. On the contrary, I believe people need to be open to developing a stronger character, becoming stronger in their self-development, practicing their technical skills longer, and developing better know-how of the actual job or career that they have chosen.

I know that is contrary to popular belief right now because everybody thinks they can become a millionaire in a minute. They think they know everything even though they're new and they're doing it on Instagram. And they're the best and they're 20 freaking minutes old. That's awesome if you worked at something for a lot of your life. I hope that you are an absolute expert and that you have perfected it. But if you just started doing it, let's be real for a minute and say this: You are probably not going to earn a barrel of cash right away. We live in a world of instant gratification and you are only seeing the highlight reel of people's lives. You don't see the hard work and the behind the scenes effort that takes place. I assure you hard work and effort are never going away no matter how sexy the highlight reels of life look.

I'm all about figuring out how to earn the most in the quickest period of time. Start your career with positivity and know that what you put out there will come back to you. Hands down, I am all about this. But, without starting from where you are and growing as a person in body, mind, and spirit, you do not deserve more. Therefore, if you have this false notion, you develop an unhealthy ego and a false sense of entitlement that will always come back to haunt you for years and years. It's unfair to yourself not to grow and develop into a well-rounded, humble person.

No seed grows up from the ground without being properly cared for. It needs the right amount of water, sun, and atmospheric pressure. Without these three fundamentals working simultaneously together, you will not have a flowering plant, let alone a garden. So why do we think as humans that we can cheat this process? In fact, without these three fundamentals—the optimal developments of your body, mind, and spirit—you will never be the best version of yourself.

If you do something well and you are good at it, keep doing it and stay in one place. Don't jump around from place to place because no one will be able to find you doing the thing that you excel in. I once heard Tyler Perry say it was like using a tiny bucket of water to water flowers in a large garden when you need a hose. You will spread yourself too thin and the flowers will barely get a sip. Make certain you stay put and keep doing your best. Harness your skill set to get better and better. Keep harnessing your best by practicing on your own time and applying what you learn. No one has ever achieved greatness without practice and putting in hard work.

Questions for Reflection:

1. How can you make what you do you better?
   (If you have been showing up without putting in the effort, forgive yourself.)

2. What are you doing for self-development right now?

3. What classes or seminars are you currently attending?

4. What have you learned lately?

CHAPTER 6

Have a Winning Attitude

Can do is where it's @
Smile more, it works. It probably helped
someone more than you know.

Award-winning attitude

If you cannot come to work every day with an award-winning attitude, why would anyone want you on their team?
I know I wouldn't.

Seriously, what do you bring to the table?

If you are not making a choice to have the best attitude
possible every day, then why are you here? I have listened to
countless interview stories of people raving about their great
attitude and professionalism. I hire them only to discover
that it was all lip service. This, of course, is something I am
not a fan of... ANYTHING THAT WASTES PEOPLE'S TIME!
I love to help people find their true potential and help them
feed their souls. But lying bullshit is something I would like
out of my life. How happy are you on a scale of 1–10 when
you walk out the door in the morning? If it's not 10, what
is up with that? Go back inside and smile at yourself in the

mirror until you feel like you're the 10 that can help others smile today.

Now, don't get me wrong. I did not start off by always having an award-winning attitude. I noticed this attitude in other people who seemed to be having all the fun and living the best lives. I used to think people were born that way or that they had a perfect life, which is why they are so happy. *You either have the best attitude or you don't.*

I always wanted to be better and make a positive impact. But I didn't realize that there was anything I could do except pray, daydream or wish about it. Until one day I had a client tell me about this book called *The Secret* (she heard about it on *the Oprah Winfrey Show*). The key message of this book is, *if you are listening, the universe always provides everything you need.* Whether you are conscious of this principle or not, it is always working, just like gravity. No one ever walks around complaining about gravity. They just accept it as an **absolute truth.**

I went right over to the bookstore that night after work and bought both the book and the movie. I was so excited to watch the movie, I almost couldn't contain myself. I was so impressed with myself as a girl who grew up wishing she could get through a book without starting another one. Thankfully, the book was laid out in a simple format I could read and get through in just a weekend.

I have since discovered about myself that it is good to read many books at a time because I learn a lot. I have learned to believe in myself, have a positive attitude, and not give in to believing dyslexia is limiting my true genius in any way. If I can do it, you can do it! Decide today that an award-winning attitude is what you want and just do it!

Do something different than you usually do. Go through your contact list and get in touch with everyone you connected with this week! Say, "Hi, how is it going?" Also, speak about whatever you love about your business—your current salon, favorite restaurant, and the accountant that you visit. What do you dislike about them? What are two things you can improve upon?

Say, *Do it now* and just do it!

Have a great attitude.
Help people and love people!

Through all of my many challenges, I have been so blessed and thankful throughout my career as a hair artist, educator, coach, mentor, salon owner, entrepreneur and now author to have so many great coaches, mentors and supportive people cheering me on. Be grateful for everything. Never let it go to your head. Remain humble but enjoy the self-esteem lift. It is so great to work hard at something you love and have people telling you you're the greatest.

As a hair stylist and service provider, I can't think of many other jobs where you are told how awesome you are all day—actually, it is every half hour on the hour, all day. Say, "Thank you," enjoy it for a moment and then get over yourself. You have more people to take care of who need your undivided attention.

Take care to ensure your self-worth is not attached to what others think of you. Make sure your self-worth is attached to what **you** think of **you**. You gotta love yourself first because if you don't, why would anyone else want to? Shine your light bright. You are going to need it. Believe in yourself. You can do anything and no one, I mean, no one is worth dimming your light for.

Remember, everyone is either your student or your teacher. Some people are both. Remember to show respect for both your student and your teacher. Sometimes, you have to be more than anybody around you! Your positive attitude and energy have to be more than the bad attitude or negative drain of others around you. My youngest son has this natural charismatic ability to make everyone in the room smile. Sometimes, people love it and sometimes people can't take it. Or they don't know what to do with it because they are not used to someone being that happy all the time.

My son knows instantly how to make people smile and how to bring an award-winning attitude to church, grocery shopping, vacation, cleaning up the house, etc. I am often in awe of how he instinctively knows this. I watch him sometimes and think, *Wow! How do we learn to be more like Christopher?* He is so good at praising the little things in a genuine way and that makes everyone he meets fall in love with him. My other son Dominic is the opposite. He quietly observes what's going on and doesn't say much. Then when he does speak, it's usually the sweetest, kindest thing and he melts your heart that way. He genuinely cares about being good and seeing good in others. I have already learned so much from motherhood it's unbelievable! It is truly unbelievable how much these kids teach us. I often ask myself how can I preserve these two qualities as they grow? To ensure that life doesn't dim that bright light they both have.

Talk to people. Enjoy people. Celebrate people. Who knows, you might be that only sparkle of light they've encountered all week. Listen to them attentively and make them feel comfortable. Tell your boss, your mommy, your friend, your employee specifically what they did well—even when you don't think it is significant. Make sure it is a genuine compliment, not something generic in nature—the more specific, the better! I have never met anyone who has ever said, "Wow, stop; I am just too appreciated." Have you? Most people need more appreciation in their life. In fact they are starving for it. So be generous and give a genuine compliment when you see it.

Smile even if you don't feel like it. Smile and smile some more. You will catch on and be happy because you are smiling and it feels good. Thus, you will feel better even if you don't want to. If you want to have an award-winning attitude, ask yourself, *What do winners do? Am I doing that at least 90 percent of the time?* If you're not, then make the needed adjustments. If yes, then keep up the good work! You rock! You are truly inspiring me! I really appreciate seeing your smile. It makes me want to smile back big and bright.

Do things that keep your energy up! What lights you up? Do you like to spend time with people who whine and complain all day? Let me guess, that's a NO! I don't either. In fact, I want to run and scream, *Stop! I do not want any of that gooey funk you are slinging my way. Stay back! You are not welcome. Alert—get away from me! Help! I love you but I need to love you from afar today because I do not want to catch any of that down and out complaining funk.*

Whenever there is a problem (and there will be problems!

It's not if, it's when), ask yourself what are **three** possible solutions? If you need help sorting this out, write it down and look at it on paper. It will make any problem appear so much smaller and more manageable. Do not throw gasoline on the fire and aggravate the problems into bigger issues by creating a whole burning forest. When you want to complain to your co-worker, your boss, your manager, or even your mother or partner, always come prepared with three possible solutions. If you don't offer tangible solutions, you just sound like a complaining whiner. Who enjoys that?

Express gratitude! I have never met anybody who could be grateful and complaining at the same time. Have you? If you struggle here, be more grateful and express more gratitude until you find a way to overturn your negative complaining all the way around to the positive side of life. There are always different ways to look at the same thing. Look at problems differently.

Pick one thing to be grateful for—any one thing and write it down. Try something easy like, *I am so grateful that I woke up today! I am so grateful I smiled all day and didn't punch any mean people in the throat today! Yay! Me!* I suggest getting a gratitude notebook or journal and writing things down that you are grateful for when you are in a good mood and refer to it often when you find yourself entering the "Negative Nelly Zone." Do this practice daily to make a maximum impact on your happiness in life. Your family, friends, and co-workers will appreciate it as well.

Here are some examples of things I am grateful for that I include in my gratitude journal. I am always grateful for these. They are my daily mantras.

I am grateful:

- for the sunshine
- for my healthy family
- for my loving and supportive family
- for waking up today
- for this beautiful cup of tea
- for my talent
- for my hard-working, award-winning team
- that I get to work doing something I love every day
- that I get to help thousands and thousands of people
- for this moment right now
- for the beauty that is all around me
- that I get to go to work every day with people that I truly respect and care about.

"If you don't like something, change it. If you can't change it, change your attitude. Don't complain."

Maya Angelou

Questions for Reflection

1. What attitude are you choosing today?
2. What are some possible solutions to your biggest problems or challenges?

CHAPTER 7

Be a Team Player

Always look for ways to help out!
Ask, "What can I do?"

Have you been making deposits or withdrawals in your team relationship bank? If you are not sure, I bet you are withdrawing more than depositing and your team knows it with certainty. Being a good team player is about putting the needs of your team above your selfish needs for the greater good of everyone.

You may ask, "How does this lead to professionalism?" And I say, "If you are always self-centric, then you cannot be team-centric." A true professional will take the time to get to know what people need to create a successful team. This is true for families and households as well as business teams or sports teams.

Working together for one common goal is definitely where it's at. No one wants to be alone on an island no matter what BS we are telling ourselves. Togetherness is always better. That's the reason God designed us this way—to love, nurture, and support each other. We need connection. We crave it as humans. It is actually one of our basic human needs.

I used to think I was being a team player when I showed up and showed the team how awesome I was. Now, I know being a team player is about knowing your role on the team and doing more than your best every day. It's about putting their needs above my own and doing what is required for the team to win, not just for myself to win. No one told me this and I did not know it instinctively. When I finally got it, it was like getting hit over the head with a brick (like in those cartoons).

Let me just tell you, I was clueless until I figured this stuff out. You will ace it because you are already closer to being a better version of yourself than I ever was when I was young.

If you focus on being a person of integrity and loyalty, you will be noticed and be well liked—probably even loved–by any team. Make sure everyone on the team knows their role. If you are unclear, ask what your role is or the roles of other team members. If you haven't told your team what you expect of them and what their individual roles are, as well as their combined team role, do not be mad at them if they do not perform because you didn't guide them.

The way I see it, everyone wants to be the best they can be and contribute to their team and shine for their own talents and strengths. I hope if you are aspiring to be a business leader, then you focus first on professionalism and make sure everyone on your team knows their role.

We cannot all be doing the same stuff or nothing major would get done. At hair salons, we may all be stylists and service providers who do hair but we all have different specialties we excel at and are within our strength zone. Thus, we have different gifts to offer. Each person's contribution is unique. This is what truly makes us great. And this is how you can win awards as a high-value team.

For example I am great at doing something different every time, like a major color correction that works synergistically with your haircut to make you look and feel your absolute best. Then, someone else on our team is great at consistently delivering the same precise men's hair cut every 2 ½ weeks because that is what the guest wants and that team member is naturally good at. I love doing color and blonding services and I especially love creating over-the-top hair show style and crazy avant-garde styles. While this makes some people on my team nervous, I absolutely love it! Other people on my team love to blow-dry style and do braids and makeup, and some people even love to do pedicures and pamper feet. We all have the things that we love to do and the things that we are great at.

I am really passionate about inspiring people to lead their best life and come together as a team for our unified team vision and mission.

I am not the best at hand holding, dotting i's and crossing t's, but we have people on our team that love that stuff. They are so great at it, and we are always looking for more people like that who truly love this kind of stuff. We do our best to know our individual roles really well and figure out what our strengths are so we can put all of our people in the lanes where they will shine and truly achieve greatness.

Being a part of a team always pushes you to achieve more. When you are surrounded by others whose passion for what we are all doing motivates and excites you, everyone achieves more. If you are alone you are less likely to try something new or attempt to learn new things. We are always encouraging each other to try something new, to figure out something challenging or solve something we have been struggling with by asking our team members what is working for them. No one who ever achieved anything great ever achieved it alone. It takes a village and a team of supportive people to make great things happen.

Always put the needs of the team, and of other people, before your own. This seems pretty simple but it demands being conscious of where you are and what you can contribute. It takes people lifting each other up and encouraging good actions as well as correcting bad behavior on the spot and the moment you see it—even if you are not an owner or manager. Yes, I repeat, especially if you do not have a title or hold any type of leadership position. You don't need a title to be a leader. You just need to have passion for the team you work with and the willingness to demonstrate great team behavior.

Team members see even tiny issues earlier than managers and owners ever do. Therefore, they are required and expected to handle situations that arise or bring the issue to someone who can do something about it. As team members, we are all guardians of culture and we are all equally committed to protect it and defend it against anyone or anything that is working against it or trying to break it down, including the boss or leader. Every day every member of your team needs to be working on protecting and defending your team culture.

My team members know that they have my full permission to question my behavior just as I would question theirs. This is especially true when what I say doesn't match my actions. Of course, they know to be respectful and do it in a way that we can all learn and grow from. I extend them the same courtesy. When team members are fully committed to being the best they can be, and being a part of a strong team that they know can do a lot of good to help others as well as push them past their own comfort zones and limitations, truly great accomplishments can happen.

Teamwork is not about pushing others down so you can be top dog. Rather, it's about lifting them up higher than they ever thought they could go because we are all in this together. Even if you do not particularly like someone as a person, you still need to get along with them and function for the greater good of the team. Now, we are all human beings. So, issues will come up that need to be handled and addressed.

When we see something isn't going right or working well, we need to address it quickly. Bring it up to the person who is doing it or grab a team member who you are comfortable with and approach the other person together with kindness and respect. Do not tell anyone but the person who can do something about it. *Do not gossip*, talk badly or put down another human being. It makes you look ugly and classless and I am fairly certain you don't like when it's done to you. Please stop this now if it is the type of behavior you participate in.

Gossip doesn't help anyone. It only hurts everyone involved, including the person who is gossiping. If your words are not helpful, do not speak them. I am often in a position where I have to discuss how we can help certain team members who are struggling or have gone offside. These are necessary conversations that help our team grow stronger and protect us all against anyone who is trying to tear down or destroy our team culture. If you need to vent, it's alright to vent to your own family and friends. But don't vent to your teammates or co-workers because this amounts to gossip and it is destructive to everyone. Not everyone is going to fit on your team and that is okay. Wish them well with love in your heart and send them on their way. If you see someone getting toxic in any way, address the issue today. Don't put it off because the longer you put it off, the bigger the issue becomes. Day in and day out, gossiping and backstabbing grows worse and we all know that is not the world we want to live in! Even though they make it look fun on reality TV.

Of course, you need to always do the right thing even if you think no one is looking because *trust me when I tell you* someone is always looking. There is no point in cutting corners or behaving in lazy, selfish ways because it unquestionably hurts everyone around you. So, suck it up and do the right thing because that is what you really know to be true anyway. It is easier to do the right thing the first time than to have to fix and clean up a bigger mess later. Wouldn't you agree?

One thing I have realized over time is people either need to be liked or to be right. Please try to love yourself enough to feel secure in the fact that a healthy debate is okay among team members. It helps us all grow and develop into the best possible versions of ourselves. It is great to share your opinion with everyone else on your team. Do not worry if you are right or if they like you. Companies and people rise to their full potential when team members feel comfortable enough to voice their true opinions to better the organization. It may not always be used and applied for each project, but it will be heard and give you satisfaction as well that you spoke what was true to you.

When you confidently speak up about what you think or believe is right, everyone will respect you for it. Remind people how valuable they are. ☺ This makes the journey and the process of growing and sustaining great teams so much more fun. When everyone feels heard and comfortable to contribute, everybody wins and can achieve more. When we surround ourselves with people who inspire us to greatness, there is nothing we cannot achieve. We are always looking for what we call a triple win, which is when our team, our guests, and our company all win. When we can get the triple win, that is the best answer. I learned this philosophy from my friend Peter Mahoney at Summit Salon Business.

If I ran out into the parking lot of the nearest shopping mall or grocery store and asked the first 100 people I saw what made them know a person was excited to join their team, they would all say a person who asks good questions. It doesn't matter if they are an employee, business owner, manager or anything in between. People know you are listening and engaged with what's going on when you ask good questions. So, pay attention and ask questions. Any team will be lucky to have you and they will welcome you with open arms. Teamwork makes the dream work!

Stay away from "still" people. Still broke, still complaining, still hating and still nowhere. If you have spent more than 60 seconds complaining, then you have already lost 60 seconds of time. Take action, any action, just stop complaining!

> *"Don't find fault, find a remedy;*
> *anybody can complain."*
>
> −*Henry Ford*

Questions for Reflection

1. Do you want to be right or keep people in your life?

2. What will it take for you to be a valuable team player?

CHAPTER 8

Commit to Being the BEST!

Never Stop Learning & Growing
Make Mistakes, Learn and Then Grow Some More!

The best looks different to everyone so you might as well be the best you! One thing that has always made me feel different or weird is that I never understood why people would get up in the morning if they didn't decide to be the best at whatever they do! Unless I am committed to being the BEST version of myself, why would I even bother to get out of bed in the morning? I have never met anyone who gets up every day with a goal to be average or mediocre. That may definitely make me weird, but I am not competitive by normal standards. I have never been about measuring myself to others. I am super competitive with myself.

I have always worked on bettering my best and pushing those around me to bettering their best to be the best version of ourselves. So I would ask you again to ask yourself, *Why do I get up every morning?* I am confident that you did not say to be average or middle of the road. I have asked this question so many times when I am speaking on stage or giving talks and No one has ever stood up and said yes. Everyone always says to help others or to be the best!

I do not believe that God (or whoever you believe in spiritually) designed us to be anything less than the best possible versions of ourselves. What do you stand for? What is your purpose? I know this may seem a bit heavy but what if at 18 you asked yourself this question and started to understand part of your answer? Or if you are already in a leadership role, helping young people find their answer as early as possible.

I love the philosophy that states, "The way to win people over and grow people on your team is to find out what their hopes and dreams are, or even their purpose, and help them reach it!" How would that be for staff loyalty?

Wherever you are, and whatever stage of life you are in, commit to being the best! Be the best friend, the best employee, the best assistant, the best wife, the best mother, the best son, the best husband, and the best boss. Just be the BEST whatever and wherever you ARE! I always tell the natural leaders on my team that the best leaders are the people who start out being the best assistants or followers. I promise this is always the truth! You cannot lead anyone else unless your know how to follow or assist! The hardest person you ever have to lead is yourself. You will have to trust me on this one.

One of the most important things to being the best is failing a lot. It is the only way you get better! You also need to have 10,000 hours of correct practice to master any skill. Now what is most important here is that you practice the skill you are trying to master correctly. This is actually new for me. I was never taught to accept failure and learn from it. But the fact is, you learn a lot from failure and that is how you get better and become the best in your chosen field. It takes over 10,000 hours of deliberate practice to become great at something. Trying to be perfect and never making any mistakes makes you feel terrible about yourself and everyone around you. It makes everyone anxious, and perfection is not attainable anyway. Only progress is attainable and that is what we should continually celebrate.

You have to put in the time to learn and grow. I was taught to do my best but my natural best never seemed good enough. I would feel like a failure and quit doing things I liked because I wasn't as good as everyone else. I was never taught that failure was okay and that is how I would learn to be better. Now I know that you have to try new things all the time. Just get started and if it doesn't work, then try something else. You won't be good at everything and that's OK. In fact it's great because what you are great at and what you enjoy will become clear. The more you try, the more you'll grow.

I don't want you to make the same mistake I made. I want you to make your own mistakes. I want you to be so much better and get there faster because now you know failure is just part of the process to greatness. Embrace it. Enjoy it. It is all part of becoming your BEST!

What does being the best look like for you? Spend some time on flushing out what that looks like for you. What do you genuinely love to do? What speaks to you? What looks appealing? What feels good? What do you never want to do again? The best way to get answers to some of these questions is to get into the habit of paying attention to what makes you feel happy and go from there. If you don't know, ask people close to you if they know when you are happiest. When does your face light up and eyes sparkle with that extra special something? If that doesn't work, go out and do a bunch of different stuff and record your answers to how you feel after doing different and varied tasks. Have some fun living your life. Remember you are the one writing your life story.

You are in charge of your life and you are the only one who can design a truly wonderful life that will make you happy. Stop thinking it is up to someone else to do this for you. Get up, SHOW UP and go out and do it for yourself and for all of your loved ones. This will make you the best version of yourself and inspire others to be the best version of themselves. I often say, "Get up, put on some lipstick and get shit done!!"

Make it a point to figure out what you are naturally good at. If you already know the answer, that is great. Do more of it. My suggestion to you is to figure out what you are naturally good at and commit to being the best at it. No matter what talents and skills you were born with, or gifted with, you still have to put the work in. Even with all the natural talent and skills Michael Jordon and LeBron James have, they still both had to practice for hours to be the greatest. Only you have the power to become the best at it.

As they say, *Talent only gets you in the door. It's up to you to do the rest!* Commitment, dedication to being the best, strength of your character, and discipline will take you the rest of the way. We all know someone who has an enormous amount of potential and natural talent who doesn't do anything to feed it or nourish it. Then they never develop and blossom into much of anything, except maybe another person sleep-walking through life whining and complaining about what the world owes them, not even realizing they could have it all if they just put in a little work. I'm sure you agree that we do not need more people like this in the world. We need to inspire each other to seize the moment and be the best we can be. Isn't that the reason why we are here? Right?

I have never met a single person—adult or child—who is excited to be average. No one gets up and says, "Yay! I'm so excited to go out and be average today. Do you want to join me in doing the bare minimum?"

These are the things that move people to take action. These are the things people get excited about. *What are you passionate about? Who can you help? What is your greatest strength? What struggles have you overcome? What would help you to develop into the best version of yourself?*

Figuring out the answers to these questions and placing a high priority on what it would take for you to be the best will help you stand out from the crowd. You will get picked first by every company you interview at. You will get your dream wife, husband, or partner because being the best is attractive and exciting to be around.

If you are someone who does the hiring and developing, you will attract more top talent and keep them happily employed by being the best in your market and coaching others to be the best they can be. No one remembers a person who did nothing to push or excite them. But everyone remembers the person who encouraged them and pushed them to grow and become their best self. Be the best friend, the best employee, the best assistant so that when you grow up, you can be the best wife, mother, husband, or father.

When you attend interviews as you enter the job market, remember to gather as much information and learn more about the company or people you are interviewing with. Make sure it is the kind of place you can develop into being the best. Make sure you are encouraged to grow and gain new knowledge on a continual basis. Share with them why you want to be a part of their team, what makes them a good fit for you, and what makes you a good fit for them. Be genuine here. Never be generic or untrue to yourself here. People want to hear what you have to say. People want to see the authentic you. Stay true to you!

Stand out from the crowd by telling them what your why is. Arrive early. Be prepared. Be dressed for the long-term job you want—the pinnacle position, not the job you have currently. Have your hair done in a professionally polished way and, ladies put makeup on. Make sure your overall look enhances who you are and speaks the same language as the words you use. You have less than 30 seconds to make a good first impression. Make sure you look like the true professional you aspire to be. Dress the part for your dream job. Be *Beyond Common*!

Never show up looking sloppy like not one thought went into getting *interview-ready*. After you get your dream job, make certain the same person shows up who was at the interview. I have talked to thousands of business owners and this is their #1 complaint. Where did the person I interviewed go? That is who I wanted for the job! Be yourself and keep working towards your personal development.

Your interview day should not be your best day. You should get better daily and develop stronger over time. That is truly what thousands of business owners are looking for. This would make you stand out from the sea of sameness. You will be special in the minds of everyone you interview with. In fact, once you get this down, call me. I know people who would hire you immediately in almost every profession.

Realize now, practicing and learning discipline early are important because becoming the best only happens over time. It is a process you develop with daily discipline, not a quick sprint to the finish line. Find a way to fall in love with the lifelong process of discipline. Every little thing matters and costs you something. Some people pay now by putting in a little bit daily, which will give them a big return. Some people pay big later with regret and nothing to show for themselves at the end of their life. PAY NOW OR PAY LATER; IF YOU PAY NOW AND MAKE LITTLE DEPOSITS, YOU WILL HAVE A BIG GAIN/WIN LATER.

The #1 way to become the best is to ask questions. If you don't ask questions, you will never know the answers you seek. You have to know what to do and how to do it to become the best you. Ask questions! Pay **attention** and ask good questions. There is such a thing as a bad question even though no one wants to tell you the **truth** here. Your questions are only a waste of time if you don't listen to the answer and apply what you have learned. Keep asking lots of quality questions. This says a lot about your commitment and dedication to growing and becoming a better person.

Questions for Reflection:

1. What does being your best look like for you?

2. What gets you excited about getting up and getting your day started?

CHAPTER 9

Love Yourself–
Take Care of Yourself

Invest time in yourself every day.
Read something positive every day.
Do what you love–dance, sing, belly laugh.
Write every day.
Play and have fun.
Laugh and smile. ☺

Love yourself

Self-love means taking care of yourself first. I don't know about you, but as a young woman, I was always taught to take care of others first—that it was selfish to do what I wanted. I was taught to do and be everything for everyone else. This always left me feeling exhausted, frustrated, and empty. I even resented people I loved and cared about because of how much pressure I put on myself running errands for them and putting their needs above my own. Crazy, right?

I realize now that I am no good to anyone unless I get time for me. I need to fill up my inspirational cup, so to speak. I need to get away from all the noise and think my own thoughts. When you are single, you think this is challenging because you struggle to find the time. Then the day you become a mother, you realize that time is fleeting and you don't even have a moment to brush your hair or use the little girl's room alone. You realize that you are never getting more time so you need to get your priorities in order. Do what is really important and what really matters. OH, AND BY ALL MEANS... DO IT FIRST.

Not sure if this is helpful to you or not, but I sure hope it is. I discovered along the way that you have to carve out time for you or you will be no good to anyone else. It's like trying to pour water out of an empty vase. If it's empty, what will come out? Nothing, even if you have a heart of gold and the best of intentions. If you're not full of what you need to give, you cannot give it. So I give you full permission—woman to woman and human-to-human– to take care of yourself first. Think of it as the ultimate gift you can give to your loved ones and everyone else we are sharing the planet with.

Take care of you. Hide under your desk or in your closet. Lock yourself in the little girl's room or get lost on your way home from work. Preferably, on a beautiful day, near a park, beach or whatever you are into. Do whatever it takes to take some time for you. Get enough sleep to be your best you! Plan ahead for a great day. Eat nourishing food and move your body.

Some of my favorite *me-time* activities include:

- Walking
- Writing or journaling
- Reading inspirational stories

- Yoga
- Cooking
- Traveling
- Going to dinner with friends for good conversations
- Learning a new activity
- Taking workshops
- Getting a massage, facial or pedicures are quick ways to pamper yourself
- Listening to audio books or podcasts that nourish my heart and mind
- Singing
- Dancing
- Belly laughing

My absolute favorite me-time activity that I love to do for myself is spending time with other passionate and motivated people that lift each other up and encourage and challenge greatness in each other.

You cannot give from an empty well. If the glass is empty, what are you giving away?

Put your mask on first before you run out of air. Only then you can help someone else. Ways I love to nourish myself are meditation, writing in my gratitude journal or reading inspirational prayers, thoughts, and ideas. I also enjoy the daily debrief, which is asking yourself: What worked well today? What challenges did you have? What can you do to make tomorrow even better?

I have recently been involved with a small faith sharing group at church and this gives me much goodness in my heart. It puts a spring in my step and a song in my heart. Who knew sharing your faith and having others in your life to ask questions and compare experiences with would be such wonderful self-love. But for me, it has been glorious. Find your heart's desire or what you need to love yourself. Do not wait to make this a priority. Do it today! Your schedule will never be clear. You will always have something to do, somewhere to be or some project to finish. Schedule it now as a priority appointment or date with yourself. Make it as important as any other meeting or appointment on your calendar.

The best thing you can do for others is take care of yourself! You matter and you can be the best you. The only way you can make it possible is by loving yourself enough and taking excellent care of yourself. Even if that voice in your head tells you it's selfish to take time for you, do it anyway because you matter!

This is the one area you must not compromise because this big, beautiful, wonderful life is not a dress rehearsal. It's yours and only you can live it. You cannot delegate this to someone else and you cannot TEXT OR PHONE it in. Only you can live it!

The needs of each person are different. So whatever you need, take the time and make a list. This way, you will be sure to follow through on taking care of your most valuable commodity, YOU!

List the top ten actions/activities that make you feel good and nourish your soul. ☺

Doing the best I can

I honestly just want to keep it real with you. I am forever a work in progress. I do not consider myself an expert at any of this stuff. I am simply doing the best I can to share the challenges I face, the failures I have overcome, my knowledge, strengths, and skills to help others. I hope that I can make a positive difference in people's lives and in this world, and I can help shape young people's lives to help build them up. I would like to give them something to be proud of, teach them how to do good in the world, and be a good person—a quality person with strong character—a self-esteem lift if you will.

I try my best to do right for everyone. I help those in need. I teach people everything I know so they can be the best they can be, and I give guidance and advice on how to rise above all the chaos and noise in the world. I am not perfect. I'm a human being and I make mistakes. I don't get it right all the time. In fact, I probably get it wrong more often than I get it right. But I continue to get up and rise up no matter what obstacles and challenges are thrown my way and I suggest you do the same. I genuinely love and care about others. I care about the greater good of humankind and can genuinely say that everyone has the potential to be kind, compassionate and loving.

If we work together helping each other, the world could be a more beautiful place. It breaks my heart when people attack people for no good reason but their own lack of love or ugliness of self. It is often said that only *hurt people* hurt people. So, don't take it personally. They are just people going through something. I choose to live my life this way because I enjoy sleeping at night and holding my head up high during the day. I love you and appreciate your support. Keep it coming because this life is one wild ride.

Even in your darkest hour, if you know you have something special, keep doing it. Keep working on it, and yourself, until your hard work pays off and you realize your dream. Do you know how many people told me I wasn't good enough, smart enough, wise enough, etc.? Enough already! It was a lot, and sometimes, it did knock me off my path or make me second guess myself and what I was trying to accomplish.

I've been told too many times that you cannot get hair stylists to function as a team. They will always have a cutthroat, backstabbing, and catty attitude. You cannot get women to stop gossiping or cutting each other down. And you cannot find intelligent enough hair stylists who care about math and goal setting. And no one would care as much about their team member's chair being as busy as their own. Well, guess what? I am happy to report we live and breathe it daily in my salon company. We hire career minded service providers that love education and being a part of a team. At Lavish Color Salon we have each other's back and operate as a team that puts WE before ME! Most of our guests are happy and comfortable to go to different service providers and try new things if they need a different time or their schedule changes. Our guests appreciate that we all say hello and greet them by name no matter who usually does their hair.

Do not believe the naysayers or dream crushers. Focus on your dream and vision as your guiding star. Stay true to your north star and allow it to guide you along the way.

Unfortunately, you need to prevent any wrong beliefs

from entering your head or influencing you in any way. Keep going after what is yours even if no one understands you. One day, it will all be clear and they will all understand. Be your own bestie and support yourself in any way that you need during this time. No one else will get it and no one else can do it for you. So, show up for yourself with the love and support that only your true bestie can provide. ☺

Even when it doesn't feel like it, you will see later that you are making progress and you are learning along the way. Keep going. I know you can do it! Even if you keep falling down, keep getting back up, over and over again!

Sometimes, it will feel like you are failing, and that is okay as long as you are learning and applying what you have learned. Focus on moving forward and that is the BEST we can ask of ourselves sometimes. It's like falling forward: at least we are moving even if it's only slightly in the right direction.

Questions for Reflection:

1. How do you show yourself some love and appreciation?
2. When are you the most happy?
3. What makes you feel good when you are down?
4. Who do you like to spend time with that supports your personal vision?
5. Who lifts you up?
6. If someone were to completely support you, what would that look like? What are they doing to show support?

CHAPTER 10

Keep Meeting New People!

Referrals are GOLD!
Connect with other people. Be in the story.

Have you ever wondered how some people do it? They simply light up the room and make friends with everyone in it! I am in awe of all of you who have this mastery as a natural skill. It certainly takes genuine charisma to do it well. Full disclosure: I am not one of those people naturally.

God did not give me this gift. I had to work for it and learn it! Do not get discouraged. You can learn new skills that will make it easier for you to always meet new people. No matter what business you are in, you will always need to meet new people, make new contacts, and generate new leads for yourself and others. So, if you are not a natural lover of people, then you need to start somewhere. Wherever you are, just start.

Start by taking baby steps. I personally love being around people talking and discussing topics that we are passionate about. I get a real rush from that kind of stuff. If I am engaged in a conversation with people that are passionate and excited about a topic, I can listen and talk all day—maybe even days. This gives me great energy and provides this amazing complete loss of time. It can feel like time is standing still and I am just totally 100 percent present in the moment. I have always taken that as something wonderful, like I am connected to everyone in the room and walk away thinking, *Wow! What a great experience. I love it. That was amazing!*

If you have already found your true passion in life, then spend more time doing it. Make new friends. Invite old friends if they love it too. If not, keep trying new activities until you find it! Figure out what you love to do and go out and do it with others. This will give you the opportunity to relax and enjoy something you love and meet other people who love doing that thing too. This is where we can use technology to enhance our life and help find others who love what we love too. Find a Facebook, Instagram, Linked-In or Meetup group full of people who love what you love and join!

Now, it could be bird watching, drinking wine, bar room trivia, shopping, playing chess, photography, dancing, yoga, cake decorating, and anything in between. Go out. Take a class. Go to a meetup group or start your own. Do whatever it takes to do something you love and enjoy with others. This will ensure you are always meeting new people and will keep you connected to the world around you.

The more you stay connected to others, the more you feel fulfilled and complete. It is one of our basic human needs. We all need love, connection, food, and shelter. Even if you think you are not a people person, I assure you, to really feel fulfilled and connected in life, you need others in some capacity. Everything else is life's beautiful bonus. Even if you are shy and afraid of socialization, you need to pick something you like to do, and do it with a group!

Play a game online, and start to get to know people virtually. This is what I call baby steps. As you feel more confident to talk to others, pick something outside the home where there are people. Despite living in this world of social this and social that, the human race is deprived of meaningful human connection (again going back to one of our basic human needs). No matter how smart we get or how much we use technology to enhance our lives, we cannot use it to replace our humanness. Like we mentioned before, please do not become a tool. Use technology for the tool that it is. Let's figure out how to bridge the gap between technology and humanity.

We can never outrun this or escape the fact that we are all, in fact, humans and connected. We need each other. So, let's get back to the point here. We need to do things we love with others. If you are not sure what you love, then try everything until you find it. Some people are so much better at telling us what they don't like, which is fine, but if you are one of these people, don't stop there. Even if you've tried 200 different things, do not stop until you find something you like to do. Make a list of everything that you would consider trying.

I have found that many people try doing things for others when they are not sure what they like or what they are good at. Start by attending a charity walk, or volunteer at any charity event or local school. Sometimes, when you are part of planning an event, or on the committee that puts events together, you sort of gently force yourself to meet people because you are working together to support a cause. Build a house with Habitat for Humanity or be the ticket taker at a local networking event. It will give you the chance to meet everyone as they are on their way. Doing this will help you get to know more people.

Now I guess I have always been more of a people person. When I was young, I was painfully shy around everyone but my family. I didn't know how to talk to people. I thought, *Why would they want to talk to me? What do I have to offer?* I didn't know what to say! What if they laughed at me or made fun of me or, even worse, ignore me like I was altogether invisible? I say I was always more of a people person even back then when I was shy because I loved being with people even if I just observed and took it all in. I loved sitting at the adult table listening to all the great stories my elders would tell. This is where you would always find me in the center of the action. Hanging on every word they spoke. I loved listening to the stories; to me, this was much better than playing. I loved every minute and I soaked it all up.

I can often be described as highly intuitive, direct and fast moving. Can you relate? It gave me energy to be around people. But it has taken me my whole life to figure this out. When I isolate myself and do not have much time for people, I am not the happiest version of myself.

Fast-forward to middle school. I was starting to come out of my shell and feeling a bit more confident in discovering and easing into being my true self around others. And then the whole mean girls saga started. I was made fun of, picked on, and bullied to the point where I was constantly in a state of rage that earned me countless detentions, suspensions, and even got me expelled from school for four days for fighting.

Now you may be wondering, how does this have anything to do with always meeting new people as this seems quite like the opposite? Does she even know WTF she is talking about? Well, I am not saying these were any of my life's greatest defining moments. They were more like humbling moments that helped shape me into becoming a much better person. This is more like me sharing all of my most humiliating, painful mistakes so that you can learn from them and arrive at your chosen goal faster. You can be better, bigger, and get there quicker.

Even to this day, I do not like to see someone picking on or gossiping about another person. I am always looking for the most amicable way to solve a communication problem. If you are not saying something that can help another person improve or get better, why are you saying it? The reason I am sharing this deeply personal story is because maybe it can keep you, or someone you know, from going through the struggles I did. So now let's get back to the story.

Let's plainly say that middle school and high school were a real struggle for me to get along with others. When I was in middle school and all the mean girls stuff kept happening, I would come home every day from school crying and wanting to die. My poor mother did not know what to do with me.

I wanted to have a lot of friends. I liked being a part of the action with people because like I said, even though I didn't know it then, I was a genuine people person at heart. My mother would always say, by the time I was 25, I would be able to count my true friends using my fingers on one hand, and I would say, *But wait, I want more. I am going to have lots of friends.* Let's keep it real. It turns out as always, Mom was right.

Here was how the bullying of the mean girls cycle went. Let's pick on her for one reason or another. Let's isolate her and tell everyone not to sit by her side at lunch, throw things at her when the teachers aren't looking, and put mean "kick me" signs. on her back so everyone can laugh when she walks down the hall.

Now I know I am not special and that each one of us probably has a similar story or something that made us feel picked on and less than. This happens to be my version of the same story so many young women and men face as they grow out of adolescence. It did not feel good to be the flavor of the week that everyone ganged up on and picked on. The next week, the mean girls would be all nice and act like we were all besties again, that we should act as if nothing happened, and trust that they were fully loyal and had my back.

I remember being like, *WTF, this is insanity!* But as most of us young girls and boys want so badly to fit in, you just go with the flow and take it. I remember asking myself, *Am I crazy? Is this really happening?* This unpleasant experience was even more emotionally scarring for me because I had divorced family abandonment issues and the *people person* side of my personality really needed to find my tribe. So even though I felt like I was betraying my own moral fiber, I kept my head down and didn't ruffle too many feathers. I tried my best to smile through the pain of rejection. Like a turtle, I crawled back into my shell.

I did seem to be the one out of the crew who had the most turns at being thrown out of the inner circle and picked on and made fun of. So, when it was a new week or when they were finally over making my life a living hell or what any 7th grader thinks hell would feel like, I would be invited back into the fold in some strange turn of events. Then slowly, they would present a new victim to pick on. I rarely joined because I don't like being unkind to people. I honestly love people and believe that we are all inherently good. Does anyone really wake up with the intention to ruin everyone's day? Continuously? Really?

I am not proud to say that I did join a few times because I fell victim to the pressures of fitting in and wanting to be accepted. It really makes you feel small and like the worst version of yourself. I would try to stay quiet and pretend I didn't know what was going on. You know like, "La La La, Oh, is that a squirrel?" I would hope no one would notice. I would avoid participating in the mean girls ritual and then I would be the victim again and again because I couldn't do it.

I am not proud of the fact that I didn't stand up for everyone back then because I was living in fear of being iced out again or made to feel like I was nothing of value. And simply putting my head down and sinking into my shyness does not make me a good person who stopped the bullies or stuck up for the underdog in the way I would if I could go back and do it over again.

I ended up spending the rest of my middle and high school years working as much as possible so I could grow up and be around people who didn't force me to dim my light. I actually had three jobs while I was in school so that I could start planning for the life I wanted in the future. I realized quite young that it took money to get freedom and freedom to me was being around people who would inspire me to greatness. I knew I didn't want to be like these mean girls. That was never going to be for me. I now fully trust myself as the person who will stand up for what I believe is right, and how I believe people should be treated! I even appreciate the lessons that I learned during those dark times. I know now that people who are being hurt at home are usually those who hurt people at school. I have even forgiven all the mean girls because I deserve that.

I have learned to forgive myself for the unkind things that I participated in. I have taken a lot from that time in my life and turned it into something empowering to women. Hair! Of course! And I have been teaching people that you have a choice even if bad stuff happened to you. Doing more bad stuff does not make anyone feel good.

When I first started doing hair, I was unusually shy. I was also scared that I wouldn't be good enough and no one would like me or my work. So, when my mother would ask if I was sure I wanted to do hair, I would say, *Yes!* She would then say people get really mad like if you mess up their bangs and they will yell at you. She would ask if I was sure I still wanted to do it. And I would say, *Yes. I will practice until I'm really good at it. I promise I won't quit, and people will like it. Just wait, Mom, and you will see.*

I know now that people always view me as being a people person who is extremely outgoing. But I started off as a shy, insecure and aloof little girl with my head held down. Over time, I slowly took one baby step after another and developed my outgoing nature. I am so grateful for that because it has allowed me to stay open to people and to always gather their input and ideas. This has really helped me grow in my career as a stylist, salon professional, educator, coach, speaker, author, and business owner.

Being open with people and willing to be vulnerable and uncomfortable in front of people, including my team members, has no doubt helped me develop a strong team and culture in my company. I don't know everything and I don't have to. I only need to ask the right questions, to get everyone on our team to open up and communicate on what they believe will help in any given situation. And I get to put the right people in the right roles on our team, which I love!

When you meet people and you don't know what to say, I always find that asking them about what they are interested in is what gets them talking. Don't spend your time worrying if people will like you. Dale Carnegie said, "If you want to get people to like you, show them that you are genuinely interested in what they have to say." If you spend all your time worrying in your head if someone likes you or not (like I did as a young girl), you miss the opportunity to really get to know people. Getting to know people is what truly makes life interesting. Knowing someone's story is what might move you to that next great discovery or a great invention. What would improve the quality of life for everyone?

Important takeaways...

- Be open
- Push through the fear and do it anyway
- Do it whatever it is even if you're shy or you don't feel like it

Just because someone appears to be outgoing doesn't mean they were born that way. Many people worked really hard to develop that skill. Spend time around people who are good at this and they will help you.

I have learned over the years to be more outgoing. I

didn't start out that way; I was really shy and just kind of afraid and I kept my head down. Until one day, when I had to model hunt for a huge industry hair show. I finally was in a situation where I was forced to go up to strangers and ask them if they wanted to model and have their hair cut. It sounds crazy I know, but if you don't have models that are beautiful and gorgeous and willing to cut off all their hair and let you do some crazy fun colors to their hair, then you don't have a hair show. And I wanted so badly to be a part of this great team of people that put on such a spectacular show, so I had to go get models or be fired or let go from the team.

Now, in retrospect it is kinda funny because I wasn't getting paid; I was volunteering and paying my own way just to surround myself with the best of the best in the hair and beauty industry. Traveling all over the world and asking total strangers if they want to model in your hair show will definitely get you over being shy. If you can talk to absolute strangers on the street and convince them why they should model in your show and get over-the-top, really funky, avant-garde hairstyles, then you pretty much can talk to anyone anywhere at anytime.

Sometimes, I would have to convince people that didn't even speak English and I had to learn how to communicate with them using hand motions and body language, whatever it took to get them to come model in our hair show. I learned whatever you do you can always do better, whether that was going out and getting models that were even more beautiful and gorgeous, whether that was blow- drying and finishing a model on stage just a little bit better, whether it was coloring and cutting hair just a bit better, or explaining and teaching your audience how and when to use just the right amount of products to achieve the best results. My mentors Irvine and Louise Rusk, as well as the whole Rusk team, used to say, "Hmm, now make it better!"

I learned so much during these times in my life where I was put in uncomfortable situations that allowed me to be stretched beyond the talent and skills that I had at the time so that I could reach *Beyond Common* results. I was truly blessed to be surrounded by people who had those talents and skill sets naturally, so, I paid attention and absorbed everything I could learn from them. No matter what you are doing or what you are afraid of, you can always do better; even if you only move one more inch in that direction, you can always do just a bit better. Be sure to always be meeting new people no matter what you do because that will be the essential key to achieving *Beyond Common* success in all you do.

If you learn to use the techniques I have recommended, you will avoid starving and asking, *Is this really the right career for me?* If you learn to use and apply the techniques I have demonstrated, you will get more referrals and earn up to $10,000 more per year throughout your entire career. I repeat: Adapt the principles I have shown you about meeting more people and getting referrals, you will earn up to $10,000 more per year in your career.

Here are three action steps to get more referrals and earn $10,000 more per year.

Every day, ask yourself:

1. What did I do well today? What did I not do that I know I needed to do? Be really honest with yourself here. (Remember that you are a good person. We are

focusing on your behavior here, not being critical of you as a person.)

2. What am I going to do more of tomorrow?

Or ask yourself:

1. Did I make an effort to meet five new people today?
2. Did I follow up with them to make a genuine connection with them?
3. What will I do more of tomorrow?

If you follow these three simple action steps every single day for 30 days, it will become a habit. Be sure to record your answers. You will get more referrals, and in a year's time, you will earn $10,000 more per year.

Questions for Reflection:

1. What fears have you pushed through lately?
2. What is your plan for meeting new people this week?
3. What are some other ways you could get referrals?

CHAPTER 11

Be First to . . . Help Others

Everyone remembers the first person who helped them. But they may not remember the second, third, or twenty-fourth. We are human and we tell stories about the first people who helped us out in our time of need. If you see a way to help someone, do it! Go for it! But be first because it's more memorable. If you can't be first, that's okay. Just keep helping people and making an impression because it will all come back around ☺

What is important to you? What do you stand for? What keeps you up at night?

Asking yourself these questions will lead the way to finding your own purpose and ultimately, figuring out what lights your soul on fire. Knowing what keeps you fueled with love and energy will help you to help others. And along this journey, you will find the things that you enjoy doing to help others.

If you have something you are passionate about, get out and get involved—love what you're doing and show the people you are helping that you really care. For instance, when someone gets a new promotion or graduates from school, be the first to call and congratulate them or buy them a book about success and professionalism like this one! This kind of thoughtfulness is appreciated and memorable.

When you see a friend or college student struggling, go out of your way and do something to help. Be creative. People do not always know what they need. Hence, sometimes merely moving into action is immensely helpful. Other times, just asking how you can help or what you can do is great because they will tell you exactly what they need and appreciate the help. Make it crystal clear that you want to help people because helping people feels good and we all need to feel good!

Please do not expect anything specific in return. When we have expectations about how people will treat us or thank us because of what we did to help them, we will grip too tight and not be happy with the simple act of kindness that helping people simply feels good. Try this. You will love it! Do kind things for people without any expectations in return. Do not expect applause and do not be attached to any expectations of how someone should return your favor. One of my favorite Buddhist sayings is:

"If you only do something because you expect something in return, you may want to reconsider doing it at all."

Understand and appreciate that you were in exactly the right place at exactly the right time. You know you're making a difference by helping someone. Those are the moments I love the most. When we wake up each morning and set our intention to be that kind of person. For every encounter, we get to create so many more, which is truly exhilarating.

Set out to make someone's day and really make a difference in their life no matter what they're going through. Someone could be on the verge of suicide because their husband has been cheating on them for years and has a mistress. They could find out that their father is dying of cancer or their mother has had a mental illness for most of her life. You really never know what someone is going through, but trust me, everyone is going through something. I repeat, everyone is going through something, even the strongest people we know.

There are one million things that each of us go through daily. We never know what is going on with others now even though we may not see it the way they do. When we think we know what is going on with someone, what is our perception? What is their perception? Whatever someone believes to be true is true. However, their perception of reality is flowing through their heart and mind and whichever colored glasses they see the world through. That is what truth is. We have to constantly come up with ways to help one another to overcome these challenges that we face as humans.

We need to be connected and we need to pay attention. When someone asks you for a favor, don't just refuse or blow them off. Take the time to either do it or check to see if you can do it. And if you see that something's going on, don't jump the gun and assume that it is not anything to do with you. I don't remember who said it but I know it's been said many times that every single person is battling a war that you cannot see. It's going on inside and it's a person's personal war to keep their mental state and their emotions in check. Maybe someone you know or an acquaintance just needs someone to talk to or someone to let them vent. Or it may be more serious than that, but either way, be willing to help in some way.

Being yourself is truly developing yourself in a way that helps you be the best version of you—the kind of person you can be proud of. The kind of person who shows up for other people is the first person who's there when you need them. You definitely have to first be this person for yourself. If you don't know how to be this person, think about what a best friend would do for you if you were to design the best friend of your dreams. Imagine what that person looks like for you. What does she do? What does she say? Then, be that **person**!

What are the five to ten things that you would want to do? Start doing those five to ten things for yourself. And when you start feeling really good, imagine you had a best friend who is now you taking care of you. You will feel loved and appreciated and really taken care of. That will make you feel so good and you will want to show up for others in that same way.

Now think about the best five to ten things that you would genuinely appreciate doing for yourself and start doing these things for others. Aim to make other people's lives easier. The more you do this, the better you become at it and it becomes like second nature. As you live this out, you become a vehicle of compassion and love for others. This provides you with the ability to serve and we all know it is more fulfilling to give than to receive.

If you need ideas and inspiration about what those 5 to 10 things would look like, here are some possibilities. But remember, I don't know what will work for you. This is what I enjoy, and what others I know have enjoyed. Whatever works for you is great for you. Do that. Please don't do any of these things for yourself if they don't make your heart feel fulfilled. Only do the ones that speak to you and make you feel joyful and fully loved.

I have so many things that I truly enjoy. Here are a few to get you started... getting a massage, getting a facial, getting a manicure or pedicure, writing, walking, hiking, yoga, and saying simple words of gratitude to myself. Also, I enjoy saying a great big **"no"** sometimes. The next one is gonna sound so kooky. I learned this from one of my mentors, Jack Canfield. You stand in front of the mirror and say to yourself what you love and appreciate about yourself. You do this every day for 30 days. It is one of the best things you can do for yourself.

Do something for yourself that nobody else has done for you. Consider what you are hugely grateful for, why you want something badly, or why you love yourself. As Jack Canfield says, "Get a crush on yourself, fall so in love with yourself, be the most kind loving friend that you have ever dreamed of having." I mean, have enough love and kindness for yourself and show up for yourself every day.

So many of us have tons of baggage and junk we carry around from our childhood and our past relationships. This stuff can beat us down. You cannot start from that place of feeling beaten down, not good enough or less than. You have to heal yourself first. And the only way to heal yourself is to love yourself. Love yourself fully—your whole self because you deserve it. We are all human. Forgive yourself for being human and let go of all the heavy baggage you're keeping to hurt yourself. Love yourself for being a great person because that is what you truly are. I am always saying to my team when I hear them say something negative to themselves.:"Stop being unkind to my friend (insert their name)." We need to say kind things to ourselves so that we have the mental muscle to be and say kind things to others. Would you ever talk to a friend the way you talk down to yourself? Let it all go and be present in the here and now!

I am trying to do the very best I can in this world. I will help anyone in need. I will teach and share everything I know with anyone who needs the knowledge and support. I give of myself. I will help a neighbor at every chance I get. I believe in the power of teaching a man to fish so that he can feed himself for a lifetime (not just doing it for him to keep him weak and dependent on me). I encourage you to do the same. I practice what I preach and I'm no stranger to hard work. I am not perfect. I am simply a human being who works hard at trying to give people a leg up in this life. I want to help people create a life that they can be proud of. A life well lived!

Sometimes, you have to dig deep and get to the heart of what is going on with someone on your team or even in your own family when they are freaking out or going off the rails in a particular moment. Do not ignore it and pretend it will go away because it will only get bigger if ignored. Dig it out now. If you handle things quickly and efficiently, people will know you care. Instead of ignoring behavior that you know isn't right, address it immediately. Don't let it grow big enough to take the relationship down or the whole team out. Handle things the moment they pop up. Remember what you permit, you promote.

Questions for Reflection:

1. What can you do to be there for someone?

2. How can you help before you are asked?

CHAPTER 12

Stop Lying to Yourself!

Own the truth,
not the lame story you've been telling yourself!

S tart now! I mean really right now... Stop lying to yourself!

You know when people have done you wrong and you try to convince yourself that they are good people because you see and believe in their potential? Or you do something wrong and do not own it? Or keep judging yourself about everything? This is your ego and you need to let it go. True! But what about trusting yourself and your ability to make sound decisions based on their **actions** not their **potential**, or the way you want to see them? We all want to see the good in people, and sometimes, we need to remember that people are **good** but they make **bad decisions** or do things that may do more harm than help. Disinvite these people from your life. Do it now! Seriously...right now! I will wait while you disinvite them from your life.

The craziest thing you can do is lie to yourself. You are so convinced of the story or narrative you create in your own mind that you try to convince yourself and anyone else who will listen to your bullshit story. Getting people to agree with your story doesn't make it true. It just makes you a great story teller and great salesperson.

Stop lying to yourself about it being easy or waiting un-til you feel like it. Simply because everyone else is doing it doesn't make it right. We all know that drinking four 64oz. Cokes every day isn't healthy and none of us should do it. But if you lie to yourself and listen to all the bullshit around you—it's on sale if you buy more, you get free refills if you buy the biggest size—you will succumb to the lie. Ignore the universal message: **Everyone is doing it because it's on special, so you should too**. None of this is healthy or smart and we are all lying to ourselves. Stop lying to yourself about it being easy. It's going to be hard! Instead, take the time to stop and wake up and think for a minute. How much Coke is really healthy for anyone? Really?? Wake up!

Stop lying to yourself if you think you are going to be good at anything without practice. Don't think someone else will practice for you. Even the best in every industry needs to practice to become the best and then practice even more to stay the best. Stop lying to yourself if you think that what got you to this point will get you to where you **want** and **dream** of going next. It takes new skills, new mindset, and courage to move past your fears and do it anyway. Oh, and in case I haven't told you yet, you will never feel like it because if feeling like it was all that it took, you would have already done this. Remember, what got you here is not going to get you where you're trying to go next. So just do it anyway!

Stop lying to yourself if you think someone is going to love you if you do not love yourself. Showing people how well you treat yourself will set the tone for what it takes to step up and love you the way you need and deserve to be loved.

Consider that how you treat you is how you train others to treat you. I think it was Tony Robbins that said, "You will always get your standard. Raise your standards, and you will effectively change your life." You have the power to attract the right people into your life, and if you believe anything different, then you should know that I love you but you are still full of shit and lying to yourself.

If you think you need to do everything perfectly before you move forward, you need to stop lying to yourself. I have been guilty of this mindset most of my life and it is a daily uphill battle to overcome. But by allowing myself to make mistakes, stumble, and fall, I've learned more than in all the planning, perfecting, and procrastinating I've ever done. Just take the first step. Make the first move. Telling myself I am more than enough is way more productive than constantly trying to perfect something before I could even get started and never move forward or get anywhere.

As we said in an earlier chapter, sometimes, you have to allow yourself to feel it! Don't run away or get a big head about it. You need to feel things to teach yourself that nothing will hurt you more than the stories you make up in your own head. Allow yourself to feel hurt, angry, sad, excited, happy, and on top of the world. Life is about living and that includes a full range of all of our human emotions.

We all naturally seek pleasure and avoid pain. What we view as joy or pain is what makes us all so different. Examples include: *I feel jealous or unloved because someone I love very much didn't meet my needs and expectations.*

Instead of creating some big story in your head about why they don't love you and who they love more, follow these simple steps:

1. Stop!
2. Take a huge deep breath.
3. Ask yourself why you are feeling that way.
4. Feel the actual emotion, whatever it is. A lot of yucky stuff may come up here and that is okay. Write it down and deal with it.
5. Deal with it and face the facts about it; there is no judgment on good or bad here. It just is.
6. Get help if you need it.
7. If in the end you desire a different result, make whatever changes necessary to get the result you desire. Repeat until you get desired results!

That is why we can all be the best versions of ourselves without fear that, by doing this, we are taking from someone else. There is abundance for all.

As I mentioned earlier, there is a true self-esteem issue at the root cause of most of our nation's problems right now. How can we elevate the self-esteem of other humans we share the planet with? What positively affects our self-esteem? We are all connected in the way that we all feel things and we are all human. Asking yourself how it feels to be, and be treated like, a true professional is an excellent way to get started. Self-discovery is what it's all about.

Being professional is about adding value to people, including yourself. It's about building others up and in turn, we build ourselves up. If we can all up our game and do that a little bit better, the world will be a kinder and better place for all of us to live out the lives we've dreamed about. We can all become the best versions of ourselves and live up to our true potential.

The Do's & Don'ts

When you are serving food in a restaurant, never say, *"Good luck"* when setting the meals down. *"Please enjoy your meal,"* is a much better idea. When you are sixteen and working at a retail store, please don't tell the women with the two wild kids in the store that your mom has the same shoes and she loves them. At a salon, never tell clients that if they tip you on a credit card, you pay taxes, and if they tip you cash, you don't. What makes you think you are too good to pay taxes? I mean, in this day and age, haven't we evolved as industry professionals?

On the following page, I have provided a list of the most important **Do's and Don'ts** that will be a great starting point for you on your success journey for both your life and career.

Do's:

- Communicate, communicate, communicate!

- Bring your whole self to work.

- Value people in a real way-at the end of the day we are all human and life is purely about relationships.

- Remember, **sense is not common**.

- Hold the door for mothers that are carrying a baby carrier with three diaper bags.

- Remember, it is your job!

- Remember that you can change if you choose to. Even if you have been asleep your whole life up until now.

- Ask if everything has been properly sanitized.

- Have your hair done by a trained professional and put on the outfit that makes you feel like a million dollars or a super hero!

- Ask for forgiveness when you need it.

- Laugh every day and find joy in everything around you.

- Remember that kindness is always in season.

- Say words of encouragement in your head or out loud if you need to or borrow my voice until you find your own. You are strong you are talented, you are smart and you are important just as you are!

- Always remember to say please and thank you to everyone!

Don'ts:

- Don't talk bad about yourself.

- Don't believe the irrational bullshit that our minds make up.

- Don't leave dust in your overhead bins; it sends the message that greatness doesn't matter to you!

- Don't expect someone else to do it for you.

- Don't think it is okay not to say hello and good bye to everyone you work with.

- Don't be an asshole-no one likes assholes.

- Don't talk bad about someone who is clearly suffering. Offer to help instead or at least ask if they need anything.

- Don't assume anything.

- Don't raise your kids the same way you were raised if you don't have the same beliefs now.

- Don't lie, cheat and steal and then convince yourself you're a good person. Because we both know you are lying to yourself.

- Don't hide your flaws or blind spots; embrace them.

- Don't forget: you are perfect as you are.

- Don't step over the pile of whatever is on the floor at work; bend over and pick it up. No matter whose job you think it is. Just bend over and do it.

I hope you have enjoyed and really learned something valuable from reading this book and taking professionalism to beyond common heights. I could personally go on and on about the do's and don'ts forever; this is my absolute most enjoyable pastime. I love coming up with and sharing stories that make people laugh. I'm sure you have many of your own and I would love for you to reach out and share them! You can find me on all forms of social media. You can send an email or you can check out my website. Please reach out in any way that serves you and let me know how I can help serve you.

Please share with me what happens in your life when you start applying these 12 essentials to living your *Beyond Common* life and the success it brings into your life and in the workplace. I wish you much success and happiness as we all work together to help elevate our individual lives and those of the communities all around us to live our lives in a truly *Beyond Common* manner. I am truly humbled and honored that you have chosen to spend time with me reading this book—I have poured my heart and soul into it for you. I hope you have enjoyed it and I hope it will serve you well as you use it as a guidebook to truly reach your absolute best version of yourself and to truly achieve what your version of success is.

Thank you and with gratitude always and forever,

Tracey Watts-Cirino

Questions for Reflection:

1. What lies or stories have you been telling yourself?

2. What can you let go of that no longer serves you?

TRACEY WATTS CIRINO

How to Connect

Everything about this book and extra Beyond Common stuff:

Connect to my universe here:

www.TraceyWattsCirino.com

Email: beyondcommon@traceywattscirino.com

Find me and Beyond Common Stories on Facebook & Instagram:

@TraceyWattsCirino
#BeyondCommon

Let's grow Beyond Common together.

Here's a list of ways to extend your Beyond Common experience:

- Video Series
- Group Coaching
- Private Workshops
- Private One on One Coaching
- Online Community
- Becoming Beyond Common is a journey. If you'd like to get help from Tracey Watts Cirino on your path to a better life for you and your family, click the link below to join the waiting list to be notified when all of our upcoming workshops and classes start. *http://bit.ly/become-beyond-common*